WORLD TALES

WORLD TALES

The extraordinary coincidence of stories told in all times, in all places

ISBN 978-1-78479-229-9

First published 1979
Published in this edition 2015

In association with The Idries Shah Foundation

The ISF Collectors' Library

Tales of A Parrot and Other Stories

The Happiest Man in The World and Other Stories

The Food of Paradise and Other Stories

The Water of Life and Other Stories

The Land Where Time Stood Still and Other Stories

This special edition of *World Tales*
is limited to five hundred copies.

Of which this is number 196.

The Happiest Man in the World and Other Stories

VOLUME II

Collected by
IDRIES SHAH

The ISF Collectors' Library

'That lurking air of hidden meanings and immemorial mythical signs which we find in some fables, recalling a people, wise and childish at once, who had built up a theory of the world ages before Aesop was born.'
— Ernest Rhys, 1925

'The content of folklore is metaphysics. Our inability to see this is due primarily to our abysmal ignorance of metaphysics and its technical terms.'
— A. K. Coomaraswamy

'The folktale is the primer of the picture-language of the soul.'
— Joseph Campbell

'They (tales) appeal to our rational and irrational instincts, to our visions and dreams… The race is richer in human and cultural values for its splendid heritage of old magic tales.'
— Dr Leonard W. Roberts

Introduction

It is quite usual to find collections of tales arranged according to language or country: *Tales of Belgium*, *Stories from the German*, or *Legends from the Indian Peoples*; some such titles must have met your eye at one time or another. It all looks very tidy, scientific even; and the study of stories is indeed a part of scholarly research.

But the deeper you go into things, the more mysterious, exciting, baffling they become. How can it be that the same story is found in Scotland and also in pre-Columbian America? Was the story of Aladdin and his Wonderful Lamp really taken from Wales (where it has been found) to the ancient East; and, if so, by whom and when? A classical Japanese narrative is part of the gypsy repertoire in Europe; where shall we pigeonhole it in national terms?

I have selected and place before you a collection of tales of which one at least goes back to the ancient Egyptian of several thousand years ago. It is presented here not to impress the reader with its age, but because it is entertaining, and also because, although the Pharaohs died out many centuries ago, this tale is recited by people all over the world who know nothing of its origins. This form of culture remains when nations, languages and faiths have long since died.

There is an almost uncanny persistence and

durability in the tale which cannot be accounted for in the present state of knowledge. Not only does it constantly appear in different incarnations which can be mapped – as the Tar-Baby story carried from Africa to America, and medieval Arabian stories from the Saracens in Sicily to the Italy of today – but from time to time remarkable collections are assembled and enjoy a phenomenal vogue: after which they lapse and are reborn, perhaps in another culture, perhaps centuries later: to delight, attract, thrill, captivate yet another audience.

Such was the great *Panchatantra*, the Far Eastern collection of tales for the education of Indian princes; the Jataka Buddhist birth-stories believed to date back two and a half thousand years; the *Thousand and One Nights*, known as 'The Mother of Tales'. Later came the collections of Straparola, Boccaccio, Chaucer and Shakespeare, and a dozen others which now form the very basis of the classical literature of Europe and Asia.

This book contains stories from all of these collections, and many more: because there is a certain basic fund of human fictions which recur, again and again, and never seem to lose their compelling attraction. Many traditional tales have a surface meaning (perhaps just a socially uplifting one) and a secondary, inner significance, which is rarely glimpsed consciously, but which nevertheless acts powerfully upon our minds. Tales have always been used, so far as we can judge, for spiritual as well as social purposes: and as parables with more or less obvious meanings this use is familiar to most people today. But, as Professor Geoffrey Parrinder says of the myth, 'its inner truth was realised when the participant was transported into the realm of the sacred and eternal.'*

Perhaps above all the tale fulfils the function not of escape but of hope. The suspending of ordinary constraints helps people to reclaim optimism and to fuel the imagination with energy for the attainment of goals: whether moral or material. Maxim Gorky realised this when he wrote: 'In tales people fly through the air on a magic carpet, walk in seven-league boots, build castles overnight; the tales opened up for me a new world where some free and all-fearless power reigned and inspired in me a dream of a better life.'

When relatively recent collectors of tales, such as Hans Christian Andersen, the Brothers Grimm, Perrault and others made their selections, they both re-established certain powerful tales in our cultures and left out others from the very vast riches of the world reservoir of stories. Paradoxically, by their very success in imprinting Cinderella, Puss-in-Boots and Beauty and the Beast anew for the modern reader (they are all very ancient tales, widely dispersed) they directed attention away from some of the most wonderful and arresting stories which did not feature

* G. Parrinder, Foreword to *Pears Encyclopaedia of Myths and Legends*, London 1976, p.10.

in their collections. Many of these stories are represented here.

Working for thirty-five years among the written and oral sources of our world heritage in tales, one feels a truly living element in them which is startlingly evident when one isolates the 'basic' stories: the ones which tend to have travelled farthest, to have featured in the largest number of classical collections, to have inspired great writers of the past and present.

One becomes aware, by this contact with the fund of tradition which constantly cries out to be projected anew, that the story in some elusive way is the basic form and inspiration. Thought or style, characterisation and belief, didactic and nationality, all recede to give place to the tale which feels almost as if it is demanding to be reborn through one's efforts. And yet those efforts themselves, in some strange way, are experienced as no more than the relatively poor expertise of the humblest midwife. It is the tale itself, when it emerges, which is king.

Erskine Caldwell, no less, has felt a similar power in the story, and is well aware of its primacy over mere thought of philosophy: 'A writer,' he says (*Atlantic Monthly*, July 1958) 'is not a great mind, he's not a great thinker, he's not a great philosopher, he's a story-teller.'

Idries Shah

Note: This is the full introduction as it appeared in the original version of *World Tales*

Contents

The Travelling Companion

A dead man whom one has helped to find rest, as a travelling companion who enables the hero to overcome trials and release a bewitched girl – this is quite as strange a plot as any. It has fired the imagination of the writer of no less a work than the scriptural Book of Tobit, and of Hans Christian Andersen, whose presentation as 'The Travelling Companion' is given here, as an example of the way in which a spare and terse legend was presented in the fiction of his time.

*The story's history also involves the ancient English romance, 'Sir Amadas', and Basque, Spanish and French country tales. It has been reincarnated in Italy as a novel (*Messer Danese*) and a poem (Brunetto's 'Constantino'). A Scottish Gaelic version has been collected by the celebrated Celtic scholar, Professor Kenneth Jackson, in Nova Scotia. Its enduring attraction is also seen in its appearance in Grimm, in the nineteenth century, and back to Straparola in*

1550, as well as in the narrations among the folktale reciters of Armenia, Scandinavia, Italy and Turkey, and among the Gypsies, Slavs, Indians and Scottish West Highlanders.

The story is here left in the form in which English presenters of Andersen customarily offered it in the heyday of his popularity.

Poor John was sorely troubled, for his father was sick unto death. They two were absolutely alone in the little room. The lamp upon the table was just flickering out, and the night was far gone.

'You have been a good son, John,' said the sick father, 'God will help you on in the world,' and he looked at him with grave, gentle eyes, drew a deep, deep breath, and died: it was just as if he had fallen asleep. But John fell a-weeping. He had now no one left in the whole world, neither father nor mother, sister nor brother.

Poor John! He knelt before the coffin and kissed the hand of his dear father. Many were the tears he wept; but at last his eyes closed, and he fell asleep with his head upon the hard bed-post. Then he dreamed a wondrous dream. He saw the sun and moon bow down before him, and he saw his father fresh and hearty again, and he heard him laugh as he used always to laugh when he was pleased. A lovely girl with a gold crown on her long fair hair held out her hand to him, and his father said, 'Look what a nice bride you've got! She is the loveliest bride in the whole world.' Then he awoke – and all this bliss was gone. His father lay dead and cold on the bed; there was absolutely no other with them. Poor John!

A week afterwards the dead man was buried. John walked close behind the coffin. He would never see again the kind father who had loved him so much.

He heard them throw the earth down on the coffin, he caught sight of the last corner of it, but the next spadeful of earth that was thrown down hid that also. Then his grief overcame him, and his heart was nigh to breaking. Those around the grave sang a hymn; it sounded so pretty, and the tears came into John's eyes: he cried, and it did his heart good. The sun shone beautifully on the green trees, as if it would say, 'Don't be distressed, John! Can't you see how lovely the blue sky is? Your father is up there now, praying to God that things may always go well with you.'

'I will always be good,' said John; 'and then I also shall go to Heaven, and be with my father. Oh, how joyful it will be when we see each other again! What a lot I shall have to tell him, and he too will show me so many things and teach me so much about the beauty of Heaven, just as he used to teach me here on earth. Oh, how joyful it will be!'

All this passed so vividly before John's mind that he could not but smile at the thought of it, though the tears were all the time running down his cheeks. The little birds were sitting on the chestnut-trees and twittering, 'twee-wit, twee-wit!' They were so happy, though they also had been at the funeral. But they knew well enough that the dead man was now in Heaven, and had wings finer and larger than theirs, and that he was now happy, because he had been good on earth, and they were quite delighted at the thought of it. John saw them flit away from the green trees far out into the wide world, and he was minded to follow their example. But first he carved a large wooden cross to place over his father's grave, and when he brought it in the evening, he found the grave nicely trimmed with sand and flowers. Strangers had done this, for they had loved the dead father.

Early next morning John packed up his little bundle, hid in his belt the whole of his patrimony – some fifty rix-dollars and a couple of silver pence – and resolved to seek his fortune in the wide world. But first he went into the churchyard to his father's grave, recited 'Our Father', and said, 'Farewell, dear Dad; I will always be a good man; and oh, pray God that it may be well with me!'

As John went through the fields all the flowers stood so fresh and beautiful in the warm sunlight, and they nodded in the wind as if they would say, 'Welcome to the green fields, is it not lovely here?' But John turned himself round once more to look at the church where he, as a little boy, had been christened; and where he had gone every Sunday with his old father and sung hymns; and he saw standing high up in one of the holes of the tower the church-elf in his little red pointed cap, shading his face with both hands, so that the sun might not shine into his eyes. John nodded farewell to him, and the little elf swung his red cap, put his hand on his heart, and kissed his fingers to him again and again, to show that he wished him well and a right prosperous journey.

John thought of all the fine things that he was going to see in the wide magnificent world, and went farther and farther away, farther than he had ever been before. He knew absolutely nothing of the towns he passed through, or the people he met – he was far away among total strangers. The first night he was obliged to sleep in a haystack in the fields, for he had no other bed. Yet it seemed very cosy to him; the King himself could not have been better off. The whole plain, with the river, the haystack, and the blue sky above it all – what finer bed-chamber could one have? The green grass, with the tiny red and white flowers, was the carpet; the elder-bushes and the hedges of wild roses were the bouquets of flowers on the dressing-table; and for his bath he had the whole river with the clear, fresh water, where the rushes nodded and said both good-morning and good-evening. The moon, high up under the blue ceiling, was a splendid large night-lamp, and it didn't set fire to the curtains, either. John could sleep quite comfortably; and so he did, and he only awoke again when the sun rose, and all the little birds round about sang, 'Good morning, good morning! Are you not up yet?'

The bells were ringing for church, it was Sunday. The people went to hear the parson preach, and John went with them and sang a hymn, and heard God's Word; and it was just as if he was in his own church where he had been christened and had sung hymns with his father. There were so many graves in the churchyard, and some of them were overgrown with tall grass. This made John think of his father's grave. It might get to look like these when he was no longer there to trim and weed it. So he sat himself down and plucked off the grass, put up again the wooden crosses that had fallen down, and put back in their proper places the wreaths which the wind had torn away from the graves, thinking to himself all the while, 'Perchance someone will do the same to my father's grave, now that I am far away.'

Outside the churchyard stood an old beggar leaning on his staff: John gave him all the little silver coins he had, and then went on his way into the wide world so happy and contented. Towards evening a terrible storm arose. John made haste to get under cover, but dark night had fallen upon him before he came at last to a little church which stood all alone on the top of a little hill. Fortunately the door stood ajar, and he crept in, and determined to stay there till the storm had passed away.

'I will lay me down in a corner,' said he. 'I am quite tired, and feel the need of a little rest.' So he sat down, folded his hands, and said his evening prayers; and, before he knew it, he was asleep and dreaming, while outside it was still thundering and lightning. When he awoke again it was midnight, but the storm had passed away, and the moon was shining through the windows upon him. In the middle of the nave stood an open coffin with a dead man in it, for he had not yet been buried. John was not at all afraid, for he had a good conscience; and besides, he knew that the dead hurt no-one; it is living wicked men who do harm. Two such living wicked people stood at that moment beside the dead man who had been placed in the church before being put in his grave; they wanted to do him harm, they would not let him lie in peace in his coffin, but wanted to cast him into the churchyard outside, poor dead man!

'Why do you do that?' asked John; ''tis an evil, wicked deed. Let him sleep in Jesu's name.'

'Stuff and nonsense!' said the two horrid men; 'he has cheated us! He owes us money which he could not pay, and now he has died into the bargain, and so we shan't get a farthing. That is why we mean to tear him out of his coffin; he shall lie outside the church-door like a dog.'

'I have no more than fifty rix-dollars,' said John; 'it is my whole inheritance; but I will cheerfully give it to you if you will faithfully promise me to leave the poor dead man in peace. I can get on well enough without the money. I have strong healthy limbs, and God will always help me.'

'Well,' said the horrid men, 'if you will pay his debts as you say, you may be quite certain that we shan't do anything to him'; and so they took the money from John, laughed heartily at his softness, and went their way. But John placed the corpse back decently in its coffin, crossed its hands, said farewell, and went with a light heart through a great forest.

Wherever the moon managed to shine in through the trees, he saw on every side of him the prettiest little elves all playing gaily. They did not mind him in the least, for they knew very well that he was good and guileless – and it is only wicked people who cannot see the elves. Some of them were no bigger than your finger, and had their long yellow hair done up with gold combs. They rocked to and fro in couples on the large dewdrops which lay on the leaves and tall grass. Sometimes the dewdrops slipped from under them, and down they fell among the long straw stalks, and then there was such laughter and uproar among the other wee manikins. It was prodigiously funny! Then they began singing, and John recognised at once all the pretty songs he had learnt as a little boy. Big speckled spiders with silver crowns on their heads weaved long swinging bridges and palaces from one hedge to another, which, when the fine dew fell upon them, looked like shining crystal in the bright moonshine; and thus it went on until the sun rose. Then the little elves crept into the flower blossoms, and the wind dispersed their bridges and palaces, which swung to and fro in the air like big spider webs.

John had just come out of the wood when a strong, manly voice exclaimed behind him, 'Hallo, comrade! Whither away?'

'Out into the wide world!' said John. 'I am a poor fellow without father or mother, but I am sure God will help me.'

'I also am going into the wide world,' said the man. 'Shall we two go together?'

'With pleasure,' said John; so they pursued their way in company, and soon got to like each other very much, for they were both good fellows. But John soon perceived that the stranger was much wiser than he; he had been nearly the whole world over, and there was nothing in existence that he could not tell you something about.

The sun was already high in the sky when they sat them down under a large tree to eat their breakfast, and the same moment an old woman came up. Oh, she was so old, quite crooked in fact, and leaned upon a crutch. She had a bundle of firewood on her back, which she had picked up in the wood. Her apron was tucked up and John saw three big bundles of bracken and willow twigs sticking out of it. When she got quite close to them, her foot slipped, she fell down and gave a loud shriek, for the poor old woman had broken her leg. John immediately proposed that they should carry her to her home, but the stranger opened his knapsack, took out a jar, and said he had a salve which would make her leg quite well and sound again in a minute, so that she could go home herself just as if she had never broken her leg at all. In return for this, however, he wanted her to give him the three bundles which she had in her apron.

'You ask a good price,' said the old woman, and nodded her head very mysteriously. She would have liked very much to keep her bundles, but it was no joke to lie there with a broken leg. So she gave him the bundles, and no sooner had he rubbed the salve on her leg, than up sprang the old granny, and went on her way much more briskly than before. A wonderful salve, truly, but you could not get it at any apothecary's.

'What do you want with those bundles?' enquired John of his comrade.

'Oh they are three pretty nosegays!' said he. 'I have taken rather a fancy to them, for I am a strange sort of fellow.' So they went on a bit farther.

'Why, how overcast it is getting!' said John, and pointed ahead of him. 'There are some terribly big clouds over there.'

'Nay,' said his travelling companion. 'Those are not clouds, they are mountains, the beautiful big mountains where one can get right above the clouds into the bracing air; and splendid it is, I can tell you!

Tomorrow we shall certainly be a good step on our journey into the wide world.'

The mountains were nothing like so close as they seemed. It took them a whole day to get to the spot where the black woods grew right up against the sky, and where there were stones as big as a whole town. A stiff pull it would be before they could get right up there, and therefore John and his travelling companion went first of all into an inn to have a good rest and brace themselves up for their journey on the morrow. A crowd of people were assembled in the tap-room, for there was a puppet-show man there. He had just set up his little theatre, and the people sat all round to see the play. But a fat old butcher had taken the front seat, which was by far the best. His big bulldog – ugh! how grim it looked – sat by his side and glared at all the company.

And now the play began, and a very pretty play it was, with a King and Queen who sat upon a velvet throne and had gold crowns on their heads and long trains behind their robes – for they could afford it. The prettiest dolls with glass eyes and large whiskers stood at all the doors, and opened and shut them continually so as to let fresh air into the room. It was quite a pretty play, and not at all sad; but just as the Queen arose and was walking across the stage, then – Heaven only knows what the bulldog was thinking about! But, anyhow, as the fat butcher was not holding him, he made one bound into the middle of the stage, and seized the Queen round the waist, so that it went 'Knick! Knack!' It was a horrible sight!

The poor man who was acting the whole play was frightened and distressed about his Queen, for she was the prettiest doll he had; and now the ugly bulldog had bitten her head off. But when all the people had gone away the stranger who had come with John said that he would soon make her all right again, and so he took out his jar and smeared the doll with salve as he had helped the poor old woman when she had broken her leg. As soon as ever the doll was rubbed she became all right again at once – nay! She could now move all her limbs about herself, you had not even to pull the string. The doll became like a living creature, except that it could not talk. The man who had the little puppet theatre was delighted. He now had no need to hold the doll at all. It could dance of its own accord.

Now when it was night, and all the people in the inn had gone to bed, somebody was heard to sigh lamentably, and kept it up so long, that everyone else got up to see what it could be. The man who had acted the play went to his little theatre, for it was from thence that the sighing seemed to come. All the wooden dolls lay higgledy-piggledy; the King and his guards were all mixed up together, and it was they who were sighing so piteously and staring with their big glass eyes, for they wanted so much to be rubbed with the ointment like the Queen, that they also might be able to move about of their own accord. The Queen sank down upon her knees, and held her pretty gold crown up in the air while she seemed to pray, 'Oh take it, take it, but anoint my consort and my courtiers!'

Then the poor man who owned the play and all the puppets could not help weeping, for it made him feel so sorry for them all. He promised to give the travelling companion all the money he took for his play next evening if only he would smear four or five of his prettiest dolls with the ointment. But the travelling companion said that all he asked in return was the big sword that hung by the man's side; and, when he had got it, he smeared six dolls with the ointment, and they immediately fell a-dancing so prettily that all the girls – the living, human girls who were looking on – fell a-dancing as well. The coachman and the scullery-maid, the lackey and the parlour maid danced together, and all the strangers followed suit, and the poker and the tongs likewise; but the last two tumbled down at the very first caper. Oh, it was a merry night!

Next morning John left them all and went right away with his comrade up the high mountains and through the large pine forests. They went so high up that the church towers far below looked like small red berries in the midst of all the green, and they could see far, far away many, many a mile, where they had never yet been. John had never in his life seen so much of the beautiful world at one time, and the sun shone so warmly from out of the fresh blue sky. He heard, too, the hunters blowing their horns among the mountains, and it was so lovely and blissful that the water came into his eyes for joy and he could not help saying, 'O God, how good Thou art! I could kiss Thee, because Thou art so good to us all, and hast given us as our own all the beauty that is in the world.'

His companion, too, stood with folded hands and gazed away over wood and town in the warm sunshine. At that moment there was a wondrously delightful sound high over their heads. They looked up into the air; a large white swan was sweeping through the sky. It was so beautiful, and it sang as they had never heard a bird sing before; but it gradually grew weaker and weaker, bowed its head, and at last sank quite slowly down at their feet, where it lay dead – the lovely bird!

'Two such beautiful big white wings as that bird has got are worth money,' said the travelling companion, 'and I mean to take them with me. Now you can see what a good thing it was I took the sword,' and with one blow he cut off both the swan's wings, for he meant to keep them.

And now they journeyed many and many a mile

across the mountains, till at last they saw before them a large city with many hundreds of towers, which shone like silver in the sunlight. In the midst of the city was a splendid marble palace covered with real gold, and there dwelt the King. John and his travelling companion would not go into the city at once but stopped at an inn outside to smarten themselves up, for they wanted to look nice when they walked about the streets.

The host told them that the King was a good man who never harmed anyone; but his daughter – God preserve us! – she was indeed a wicked Princess. She was beautiful enough, indeed no one could be more pretty and captivating than she; but what was the good of that when she was a vile, wicked witch, through whose fault so many handsome Princes had lost their lives? She had given everyone leave to woo her; anybody might come forward; whether he was Prince or beggar, it was all the same, he had only to guess three things she asked him. If he could give the right answers, she would marry him, and he would reign over the whole land when her father died. But if he could not guess these three things, she had him hanged or beheaded, so evil and wicked was this lovely Princess.

Her father, the old King, was sore afflicted at this state of things, but he could not prevent her from being so wicked, for he had once said that he would have nothing whatever to do with her lovers, and that she could do what she liked in that matter. Hitherto, every Prince who had tried to guess the questions so as to win the Princess had always failed, and so had either been hanged or beheaded, and yet he had always been warned beforehand not to woo her. The old King was so grieved at all the sorrow and misery caused thereby that once a year he knelt down all day with his soldiers and prayed that the Princess might become good; but this she absolutely refused to be, and even the old women who drank brandy dyed it quite black before they drank it, by way of mourning, for what else could they do?

'The nasty Princess!' said John, 'she should really have the birch-rod; it would do her good! If only I were the old King, she should bleed for it yet!'

But, of course, a King may not break his word, and this King had promised not to interfere.

At that moment they heard the people outside cry 'Hurrah!' The Princess was passing by, and she really was so lovely that all the people forgot for the moment how wicked she was, and so they cried 'Hurrah!' Fresh, lovely maidens, all in white silk gowns with golden tulips in their hands, rode on coal-black horses by her side. The Princess herself had a chalk-white horse bedecked with diamonds and rubies; her riding habit was of pure gold, and the whip she had in her hand looked like a sunbeam. The gold crown on her head was as if made of little stars taken from the sky; and her mantle was embroidered with the wings of thousands and thousands of little butterflies. At the same time, she was ever so much lovelier than her raiment.

When John caught sight of her, he turned as red in the face as a drop of blood, and could scarcely utter a single word. The Princess looked exactly like the beautiful girl with the gold crown whom he had dreamed about on the night his father died. He thought her so beautiful, and could not help loving her. It was certainly not true, thought he, that she could be an evil witch who had people hanged or beheaded when they could not guess what she asked them. 'Everyone, they say, even the poorest beggar, has leave to woo her; then I, too, will go up to the palace, because I really can't help it!'

Everyone said that he ought not to do so. He would certainly fare as all the others had done. His travelling companion also dissuaded him, but John declared that it would all come right, brushed his shoes and jacket, washed his face and hands, combed his beautiful yellow hair, and so went quite alone into the city and up to the palace.

'Come in!' said the old King when John knocked at the door. John opened the door, and the old King, in a dressing-gown and embroidered slippers, came to meet him. He had his gold crown upon his head, his sceptre in one hand and the orb in the other.

'Wait a bit,' said he, and he shoved the orb under one arm, so as to be able to shake hands with John. But as soon as he understood that it was another wooer, he began to weep so violently that the sceptre and orb fell upon the floor, and he had to dry his tears with his dressing-gown. Poor old King!

'Don't do it,' said he, 'it will go as badly with you as with all the others. Well, you shall see for yourself!' And so he led John into the Princess's pleasure-garden. Oh, what a horrible sight! On every tree hung three or four king's sons who had wooed the Princess, but had been unable to guess the things she had asked them. Every time the wind blew, all their bones rattled so that the small birds were scared away and never dared to come into the garden. All the flowers were tied to dead men's bones instead of sticks, and grinning skulls stood in all the flower-pots. That was a nice garden for a Princess.

'Look there now!' said the old King. 'So it will fare with you as with all the others you see here. Give up the idea, do! You make me positively wretched; I take it so much to heart.'

John kissed the hand of the good old King, and said that it would all come right in the end, for he was so fond of the lovely Princess. At the same moment the Princess herself came riding into the courtyard with all her ladies, so they went out to meet her, and said good-day. She was lovely indeed, and she held out her hand to John, who loved her more than ever. She surely could never be the evil, wicked witch that all the people said she was! They went up into the drawing-room, and the little pages presented them with sweetmeats and gingerbread-nuts. But the old King was so grieved that he could not eat anything; and, besides, the gingerbread-nuts were too tough for his teeth.

It was now arranged that John was to come up to the palace again next morning, when the judges and the whole Senate would be gathered together to hear how he got on with the guessing. If he got through with it, he was to come twice more, but hitherto there had never been anyone who had guessed the first time, and so they had all lost their lives. John was not a bit anxious as to how he should fare; he was in the best of humours, thought of nothing but the charming Princess, and believed firmly that God would help him somehow but how he had no idea, nor would he even bestow a single thought upon it. He actually danced along the highway as he went back to his inn, where his travelling companion awaited him.

John could not find words to express how nice the Princess had been to him, and how beautiful she was. He longed already for the next day to come that he might go to the palace again and try his luck at guessing. But his travelling companion shook his head and was very sad.

'I am so fond of you,' said he, 'and we might have been companions together for a long time to come yet. Poor dear John! I could weep my eyes out, but I won't spoil the last evening, perhaps, that we shall ever spend together. We will be merry, right merry. Tomorrow when you are gone I shall have cause to weep!'

All the people in the city had immediately got to know that a new wooer had arrived, and accordingly there was great lamentation. The theatre was closed, all the cake-women tied pieces of crape round their sugar-pigs, the King and the priests knelt in the church. There was such a lamentation, for how could it possibly fare better with John than with all the suitors who had gone before him? Towards evening the travelling companion brewed a large bowl of punch and said to John that they would now be jolly together and drink the Princess's health. But when John had drunk two glasses he became so drowsy that he could not keep his eyes open, so he fell fast asleep. The travelling companion lifted John very softly from the chair and laid him on the bed. And when it was night and quite dark, he took the two large wings which he had cut off the swan, bound them tightly to his shoulders, put in his pocket the largest of the bundles of birches which he had got from the old woman who had fallen and broken her leg, opened the window and flew away over the city straight to the palace, where he crouched down in a corner just under the window which looked into the Princess's bedroom.

The whole city lay in silence when the clock struck a quarter to twelve. Then the window flew open and the Princess flew out in a large white cape, and with long black wings, right across the town to a large mountain. The travelling companion made himself invisible, so that she could not see him at all, flew behind her, and whipped the Princess with his birches till he drew blood. Ugh! that was something like a flight through the air! The wind caught her cape, so that it bulged out on all sides like a huge sail, and the moon shone through it. 'How it hails! How it hails!' said the Princess at every blow she got from the birches, and she had quite enough of it too!

At last she came right up to the mountainside, and knocked. There was a rolling sound like thunder, while the mountain opened and the Princess went in, the travelling companion following after, for no one could see him – he was invisible. They went through a large, long passage where the walls sparkled most wondrously; there were thousands and thousands of red-hot spiders there that ran up and down the walls and glowed like fire. And now they came to a large room built of gold and silver. Flowers as large as sunflowers, red and blue, gleamed on the walls; but none could pluck these flowers for their stalks were nasty, venomous serpents, and the blossoms were the flames that came out of serpents' mouths. The atmosphere was all full of shining glow-worms and sky-blue bats, which flapped their gossamer wings to and fro.

It was indeed a strange sight. In the middle of the floor was a throne supported by four skeleton horses, with a harness of fiery-red spiders. The throne itself was of milk-white glass, and the cushions were small black mice, which bit each other in the heel continually. Above the throne was a canopy of rosy-red spider webs, sewn with the prettiest small green flies, which sparkled like precious stones. In the midst of the throne sat an old Troll, with a crown upon his hideous head and a sceptre in his hand. He kissed the Princess on the forehead, invited her to sit down beside him on the gorgeous throne, and then the music began.

Big black grasshoppers played on the Jew's harp, and the owl beat his stomach with his wings to supply the place of the drum. It was a ridiculous concert. Wee, wee pixies with will-o'-the-wisps in their caps danced round and round the room. No one could see the travelling companion; he had posted himself right behind the throne, and heard and saw everything. The courtiers – for they also now came in – were smart and distinguished-looking; but anyone who had eyes to see could perceive soon enough what sort of people they were. They were neither more nor less than broomsticks with cabbage-heads on, who had come alive by the magic spells of the Troll, and they were dressed up in fine, brocaded garments. But that didn't matter a bit – they were only there for show. So there was a little dancing, and after that the Princess told the Troll that she had got a new wooer, and therefore wanted to know what question she should put to him when he came up to the palace next morning.

'Listen!' said the Troll, 'and I'll tell you. You must choose something very easy, and then it will never occur to him. Think of your own slipper; he won't guess that. Then have his head cut off! But don't forget to bring me his eyes, for I want to eat them!'

The Princess curtsied very low, and said she would not forget the eyes; then the Troll opened the mountain, and she flew home again. But the travelling companion followed after and flogged her so vigorously with the birches that she groaned at the violence of the hailstorm, and hastened as fast as she could to her bedroom again through the window. Then the travelling companion flew back to the inn where John was sleeping soundly, unloosed his wings, and laid himself down upon the bed, for he was very tired, to say the least of it.

It was quite early in the morning when John awoke. The travelling companion rose at the same time, and told him that he had dreamed a very strange dream that night, about the Princess and one of her shoes, and bade him therefore ask, when it came to the point, whether the Princess had not thought of one of her own shoes. This indeed was what he had heard from the Troll in the mountain; but he would not tell John anything about that, but simply bade him ask if she had not thought of one of her slippers.

'I may just as well ask about that as about anything else,' said John; 'you may perhaps have dreamt the right answer after all, for I believe that God helps me at all times. At the same time, however, I will bid you farewell; for if I guess wrong, I shall never see you more.' So they kissed each other, and John went off to the city and up to the palace.

The whole of the grand saloon was quite full of people. The judges sat in easy-chairs, and they rested their heads on eider-down cushions because they had so much to think about. The old King stood up and dried his eyes with a white pocket-handkerchief. And now the Princess entered; she was even lovelier than yesterday, and saluted them all so sweetly. To John she gave her hand, and said, 'Good morning to you!' And now John had to guess what she was thinking about. Heavens! How kindly she looked; but the instant she heard him say one word, 'slipper', her face became chalky white, and she trembled in every limb. But it profited her nothing, for he had guessed rightly.

Bless me! how glad the old King was. He cut capers till the boards rocked again, and all the people clapped their hands for him and John, who had thus guessed rightly the first time. The travelling companion beamed with joy when he heard how well it had all gone off; but John clasped his hands and thanked God, Who, he felt sure, would help him the two remaining times. The second guessing was fixed for the following day.

The same thing happened that evening as on yesternight. When John fell asleep, his travelling companion flew after the Princess into the mountain, and flogged her even harder than the first time, for he took two bundles of birches with him on this occasion. Nobody could see him, and he heard everything. The Princess was to think of her glove, and he told this to John just as if he had dreamt it again, so John was able to guess aright – and oh, what joy there was in the Palace! The whole court cut capers just as they had seen the King do the first time, but the Princess lay upon the sofa and would not say a single word.

Now all depended upon whether John would guess rightly the third time. If things went well, he was to have the lovely Princess and inherit the whole kingdom when the old King died; but if he guessed wrongly, he would lose his life and the Troll would eat his beautiful eyes.

The evening before John went early to bed, said

his prayers, and then dropped off into a sweet sleep; but the travelling companion bound the wings to his shoulders, fastened his sword by his side, took all three bundles of birches with him and then flew to the palace. It was a pitch-black night.

The storm raged so that the tiles flew from the roofs of the houses, and the trees in the garden where the skeletons hung swayed to and fro like reeds in the blast. The lightning flashed every moment, and the thunder rolled till it seemed like a single peal lasting through the livelong night. And now the window sprang open and the Princess flew out. She was as pale as death, but she laughed wildly at the bad weather – it didn't seem rough enough for her – and her white cape whirled round in the air like a huge sail. But the travelling companion scourged her with his three bundles of birches till her blood dripped down upon the ground, and she could scarcely fly any farther.

At last, however, she came to the mountain. 'How it hails and blows!' she cried; 'never have I been out in such weather before!'

'Yes,' said the Troll. 'One may have too much of a good thing!'

And then she told him that John had guessed aright the second time also. If he did so again on the morrow, victory would be his, and she could never come out to the Troll in the mountain again, and would never be able to practise her enchantments as heretofore, whereupon she was sore distressed.

'He will not be able to guess this time,' said the Troll. 'I will find something the thought of which has never entered his head, unless he be an even greater magician than I am. But now, let us be merry!' and with that he took the Princess by both hands and they danced round and round with all the little pixies and will-o'-the-wisps that were in the room; and the red spiders ran up and down the walls with equal glee; the fire-flowers glowed and sparkled, the owl beat the drum, the crickets piped, and the grasshoppers blew upon their Jew's harps. It was a right merry ball. When the dance had lasted some time, the Princess declared that she must go home or she would be missed at the palace. The Troll said that he would go with her, so that they might have a little more time together.

Away they flew through the bad weather, and the travelling companion beat his birches to shreds on their backs. Never had the Troll been out in such a hailstorm. Outside the palace he bade the Princess farewell, and the same instance he whispered softly to her, 'Think of my head!' But the travelling companion heard it all the same, and at the very moment when the Princess glided through the window to her bedroom, and the Troll was about to turn back again, he seized him by his long black beard and hewed off his hideous trollish head close upon his shoulders with his sword before the Troll himself was aware of it. He hurled the body down into the sea for the fishes, but the head he merely dipped once or twice in the water, and then he tied it up in his silk pocket-handkerchief, and took it home with him to the inn, and laid himself down to sleep. Next morning he gave the pocket-handkerchief to John but told him not to unloose it till the Princess herself asked him what it was she was thinking of.

There were so many in the grand saloon in the Palace that they stood as close together as radishes tied up in a bundle. The council sat in their chairs with the soft cushions, and the old King had new clothes on, and his gold crown and sceptre had been well furbished up for the occasion and looked splendid; but the Princess was quite pale, and had on a coal-black dress, just as if she was going to a funeral.

'What have I been thinking of?' said she to John, and straightway he loosed the pocket-handkerchief, and was quite terrified himself when he saw the hideous Troll's head. Everyone shuddered, for it was indeed a terrible sight; but the Princess sat there like a stone statue and could not utter a single word.

At last she got up and gave John her hand because he had guessed aright; and there was no denying it. She looked neither to the right nor to the left, but sighed from the bottom of her heart and said: 'You are now my lord and master! This evening we will celebrate our wedding!'

'I don't object,' said the old King; 'we would have it so!'

All the people then cried 'Hurrah!' The guards on duty played music in the streets, the bells rang, and the cake-women took the crape off their sugar-pigs, for the joy was universal. Three oxen roasted whole and stuffed full with geese and pullets were placed in the middle of the market-place, and everyone could come and help himself. The fountains were running with wine of the best sort; and everyone who bought a halfpenny roll at the bakers received six large buns into the bargain, and buns with raisins in them, too!

In the evening the whole town was illuminated, and the soldiers fired their guns, and the boys let off crackers, and in the palace there was no end of eating, and drinking, and toasting and dancing, and all the fine gentlemen and lovely young ladies danced with each other, and you could hear them singing ever so far off.

But the Princess was still a witch for all that, and cared not an atom for John. The travelling companion did not forget this, and he therefore gave John three feathers from the swan's wings, and a little flask with some drops in it, and he told him to place by the side of the bridal-bed a large vat full of water, and just as the Princess was about to get into bed, he was to give her a little shove so that she should fall into the water, when he was to duck her three times, taking care first of all, however, to throw the feathers and the drops in. In that way the enchantment would be broken, and she would get to be very fond of him.

John did all that his travelling companion had advised him. The Princess shrieked loudly when he ducked her under the water, and wriggled between his hands like a huge coal-black swan with sparkling eyes. When she came up to the surface of the water the second time, the swan was white, with the exception of a single black ring round its neck. John prayed devotedly to God, and let the water gurgle for the third time over the bird's head, whereupon it immediately changed into the loveliest of Princesses. She was even handsomer than before, and thanked him with tears in her beautiful eyes for breaking her spells. Next morning the old King came in state with his whole court, and the ceremony of congratulation lasted all day.

Last of all came the travelling companion, staff in hand, with his knapsack on his shoulder. John kissed him again and again, and said he must not go away, but must stay with him for all his good fortune was owing to him. But the travelling companion shook his head, and said to him very gently and kindly, 'Nay, for my time is now up. I have only paid my debts. Do you recollect the dead man to whom evil-doers would have done a mischief? You gave all you had that he might have rest in his grave. That dead man is myself!' and he straightaway was gone.

The wedding lasted a whole month. John and the Princess loved each other dearly, and the old King lived many happy days and let their wee, wee children ride-a-cockhorse on his knee and play with his sceptre; but John reigned over the whole realm.

The Riddles

Over the centuries tales have migrated widely, and have been used by nationalists, followers of creeds and followers of individuals, to support their cause or interest. Hence the same tale is told of Mullah Nasrudin in Iran and of Ivan the Terrible in Russia; of Buddha and of a Christian saint; of William Tell in Switzerland and about Mongol and other heroes. Although the original intention may have been to strengthen the creed or individual (or even accidental adoption), the price paid has sometimes proved to be rather high. When the tale is shown to have been known before the date of the supposed exploit, great disappointment can set in. Almost the only recourse for those wanting to continue to believe that, for instance, the Arthurian 'sword in the stone' incident was original in Britain was to claim polygenesis: 'multiple and independent invention in different places through coincidence of thought'. The Nordic and Mongolian accounts of wonderful swords could thus be accounted for, as well as the Arabian narrative of Antar the Mighty, and the similarity to the legends of the staff of Moses among the Jews.

Substantially, the following tale – on the Riddle Theme – is found both in the eleventh-century Welsh and also in India of about two thousand years ago. It must be one of the most widespread conceptions, for examples have been collected from every part of Europe, as well as in Arabia, Africa, Mongolia and the Philippines. Clever girls killing demons and marrying kings, not to speak of magical deaths and the effect of unusual circumstances, are clearly of the greatest intercultural attraction.

This version is found in Turkestan, where the Russian, Turanian and Iranian ethnic groups meet.

THERE WAS A time, and there was not a time, when the sky was green and the earth was a thick stew – there was a King in the mountain fastness of the Pamir Mountains, on the borders of China, India and the God-Given Kingdom of Afghanistan. The ruler of that kingdom was very wise, very brave and strong, very chivalrous and very rich. Everyone loved him, and they respected his justice, his mercy and his honesty.

Then, one day, he made a strange announcement; and the heralds cried it through the land:

'One must come to me, neither clothed nor naked, neither afoot nor on a horse, and speak to me neither indoors nor out. If this person comes, the country will be saved. If not, we shall all be destroyed!'

Everyone was amazed by the King's edict, and for long nothing happened, until one day a young girl said quite unexpectedly to her father, a poor firewood-collector:

'Father, I must go to the King. I know how we can be saved; and by this means we shall also be released from our poverty!'

The wood-collector was surprised, and he tried to deter her from her plan, but she would not be gainsaid, and so he reluctantly allowed her to leave their tiny cottage and travel where the King ruled.

When the girl arrived at the King's palace, she lay down at the door and cried:

'Come out, O King – for I am here to save your

kingdom!'

The King asked:

'What is that commotion?'

'Your Majesty, there is some peasant girl, shouting that you must see her, for she will save the country!' answered the courtiers.

The King went to the gate, and saw the maiden lying across the threshold:

'I am neither in nor out, and so I have fulfilled one thing you wanted,' she said.

'But', said the King, 'what about being neither naked nor clothed?' But then he noticed that she was wearing a net, which covered her and yet did not.

'I have been neither riding nor on foot,' she explained, 'because I came here dragged by a mountain-goat!'

The King told her to enter the palace, and when they were seated in the full court, he said:

'Know, O clever girl, that I am in the power of a terrible Ghoul, a supernatural demon who says he will destroy the country. But he was heard to say in his sleep that only such a person as could do the things which I announced could save the Kingdom.'

'I am ready to help,' said the girl, 'but what do I do next?'

'You must answer the following riddles,' said the King; 'they have been repeatedly cried out by the Ghoul in its ravings:

'First, how many stars are in the sky?'

'That's easy,' said the maiden, 'as many as there are hairs in a ghoul's head. This can be confirmed by plucking them out as you tell off each star, one by one.'

'Very well,' said the King, 'I shall tell him. But now to the next question:

'How far is it from here to the end of the earth?'

The girl at once answered:

'Just as far as the return journey from the end of the earth to here!'

'Very well,' said the King, 'I shall tell the Ghoul. But now to the last question:

'How high is the sky?'

The girl said:

'There is no difficulty with that question. The sky is as high as a Ghoul can kick itself. It is welcome to try, if it does not believe me!'

'Very well,' said the King, 'I shall tell the Ghoul.'

The Ghoul returned from a hunting expedition a few hours later, and it said to the King, in a voice like thunder:

'Stupid King! Have you the answers to the riddles of vulnerability yet?'

The King told him what the maiden had told him.

The Ghoul was furious.

'Those are the right answers; but you still have to pass the final test. This is concerned with the method of killing me! I am to be killed only by someone who is neither man nor beast; by someone who does it neither by day nor night; someone who offers me a present which is not a present; neither by metal nor rope nor poison nor stone nor fire nor water; one who is neither eating nor fasting at the time.'

And the Ghoul then went up into a huge tree to sleep, for he was gorged with food from his hunting. He raved away in his sleep in quite an alarming manner.

The King reported the conversation to the wood-collector's daughter.

'Nothing simpler,' she said, 'I shall start very soon.'

Then when it was twilight – neither day nor night – she went to the bottom of the tree where the Ghoul was sleeping and shouted:

'Wake up, Ghoul, for your last moment has come! I am a woman – neither man nor beast. It is neither day nor night. Here is my present which is not a present!'

And she held out a bird. When the Ghoul tried to take it, it flew away. The Ghoul realised that this gift was indeed not one.

'But you must be either eating or fasting!' it roared.

'I am doing neither – I am chewing a piece of bark!' the maid shouted back.

And, as she said these words the Ghoul, overcome by rage, toppled to the ground. He was not killed by sword or spear, by rope or arrow, by poison or by anything else other than his own fury which caused him to fall to the ground, where his tremendous weight smashed him to death.

'Now,' said the King, as soon as everyone had stopped shaking from the earth-tremor which the impact had caused, 'tell me one last thing, maiden: what am I thinking?'

'That I am so clever and attractive that you will marry me!' said the girl.

And she was right; so they were married and they ruled the land together for the rest of their long and happy lives.

The Grateful Animals and the Ungrateful Man

This Tibetan tale, taken from Indian sources by Anton von Schiefner, is supposed to inculcate a Buddhist message that animals are reincarnated people. But the underlying idea, that animals are all better than some people, has been seen by some observers as showing this to be a survival of an animal-worship tale, incorporated incompletely into the Buddhist atmosphere. The story travelled westwards through the Indian Panchatantra *collection in Sanskrit, of about 750 AD, into the Syriac* Kalilag and Damnag *and then into the Arabic version of the same anthology. From there, about 1080 AD, it was put into Greek by Symeon Seth. The Latin translation, through the Hebrew, was made by Johannes of Capua in the 13th century; and from that book it was diffused into Spanish, German, French, Italian and English. Hence the story has a traceable literary ancestry far more complete than the majority of world tales.*

The great King Richard (the Lionhearted) is recorded as having often related a version of this tale after his return from the Crusades. It was certainly current in Palestine when Richard was there; so Matthew Paris, a monk of the Abbey of St Albans, was probably correct in this assertion, which he wrote in his Chronicle in 1195 AD, four years before King Richard died.

In very ancient times, King Brahma-Datta was on the throne of Varanesi, in India. One of his subjects was a man who went into the forest, with his axe, to chop wood; but while he was there he was chased by a lion, and fell into a pit. The lion, who wanted to eat him, fell in as well; and so did a mouse which had been pursued by a snake. A falcon swooped on the mouse, but he got caught in the pit as well, entangled in the undergrowth.

Their natures did not change when they found themselves trapped in this way, and all the predators wanted to kill, while the others were desperately anxious to escape.

The wise lion, however, said to the animals:

'You, honoured ones, are all my comrades. As things are at the moment, we are suffering intolerable distress through suffering. Let us not, therefore, expose one another to danger, but sit patiently without disturbance.'

Now, fate so decreed that a hunter should be in the area, seeking gazelles, and came across the place where the animals were trapped. As soon as they realised that he was there, they shouted to him to save them.

The hunter understood what had happened, and first of all helped the lion out of captivity. The great beast touched his feet in homage and said:

'I shall show my gratitude to you in due time.

But do not draw out the black-headed one' – the man, who of course had black hair – 'for he forgets kindnesses done to him.'

The hunter set the other creatures free; and they, too, expressed their gratitude to him. And he went on his way.

On another occasion, the hunter came to the place where the lion had killed a gazelle, and the animal touched his feet and gave the game animal to him.

It so happened, some time afterwards, that the King Brahma-Datta had gone into the park with his wives and, after enjoying himself there, fell asleep. The ladies took off their clothes and roamed about the park, put aside their jewels and sat at ease, and generally relaxed. Now, one of the women had put her jewellery down and fell asleep. The falcon, which had been keeping an eye on everything on the ground, swooped down, took up the gems, and flew with them to the hunter, to whom he presented them.

Presently, the King and his womenfolk awoke and returned to Varanesi; but one of the wives said to her husband, 'O King! My jewels have been lost in the park.'

The King gave orders that the missing objects should be found, and his ministers made the fullest enquiries. Word reached the black-headed man, who sometimes visited the hunter and knew that he had the ornaments, and how he got them. With ungrateful heart, he went to the King and told him about this.

The King was very angry. His men visited the hunter and said: 'We know that you stole the Royal ornaments from the park.' The hunter was very frightened, and tried to explain what had happened, telling the whole story. But he was put in chains and thrown into prison.

The mouse, however, came to know of what had happened. He went to the snake and said, 'Our benefactor, the hunter, through the evil of the black-headed one, has been cast into prison, what can we do?'

The snake said: 'I shall see the hunter.' He went to the hunter in his prison and said: 'Today I will bite the King. As soon as it is known that this has happened, you will offer to cure him. When he accepts, you will use this special remedy. If you do that, there is no doubt that the King will, as a reward, free you, and make you valuable gifts.'

So the snake bit the King, and the hunter cured him, and the King had him released, and made him many presents.

The Value of a Treasure Hoard

'Tales have wings,' said Isaac D'Israeli, 'whether they come from the East or from the North, and they soon become denizens wherever they alight.' The Chinese story which follows, from a Hong Kong collection, is almost literally paralleled in a tale attributed to Laird Braco, an ancestor of the Earls of Fife, in Scotland, who was a miser, and, one day, showed a farmer his hoard. There are many cognates, in as differing settings as the Sufi tales of Persia and a recent one of the American millionaire who paid a colossal sum for a statue which he erected by the roadside.

Once upon a time, in China, there was a priest, who was both avaricious and rich. He loved jewels, which he collected, constantly adding more pieces to his wonderful hoard, which he kept securely locked away, hidden from any eyes but his own.

Now the priest had a friend who visited him one day and who expressed interest in seeing the gems.

'I would be delighted to take them out, so that I, too, could look at them,' said the priest.

So the collection was brought, and the two feasted their eyes on the beautiful treasure for a long time, lost in admiration.

When the time came for him to leave, the priest's guest said:

'Thank you for giving me the treasure!'

'Do not thank me for something which you have not got,' said the priest, 'for I have not given you the jewels, and they are not yours at all.'

His friend answered:

'As you know, I have had as much pleasure from looking at the treasures as you, so there is no difference between us, as you yourself only look at them – except that *you* have the trouble and expense of finding, buying, and looking after them.'

Patient Griselda

Over a century ago, a German encyclopaedia entry listed the bibliography of 'Patient Griselda' in no less than fifteen columns. The story appears in Chaucer's Canterbury Tales *as 'The Clerk's Tale', and Griselda's patience, not her husband's arguable insanity, always seem to be the point noted and stressed. Chaucer took the story from Petrarch's Latin; he in turn got it from the last tale in Boccaccio's* Decameron, *and he from a French tale, 'Parlement des Femmes'. It is found in Afansief's Russian anthology, and was also collected in one form by the Brothers Grimm.*

And yet, as Brewer's Dictionary *has it, Griselda's trials 'are almost as unbelievable as the fortitude with which she is credited to have borne them'. Griselda's husband seems a monster who took away her children and made her feel, for years, that they had been killed – just to test her. When she had been tested, they lived happily ever after. Strange though Dr Brewer may understandably find this theme, the Indian cognate, while perhaps explaining the husband's conduct, seems to raise more questions than it answers. According to the ancient* Nidanakatha *of Buddhist birth-stories, Mangala Buddha was involved in a parallel experience. A demon, disguised as a Brahmin, asked him for his two children. He handed them over joyfully. The demon then devoured the children and the Bodhisatta felt no sorrow. On the contrary, he felt rather 'a great joy and satisfaction'. As a consequence, he was almost instantly transformed into the Buddha.*

Both versions are religious; the test is administered in the one case by a husband, standing for the divine testing of humanity, in the other by a demon. In the one case the woman benefits by attaining happiness, so that her husband was really being cruel to be kind; in the other, the father (the Bodhisatta) benefits to the extent of actually becoming Buddha. Although many people of today will have difficulty in understanding the mentality of ancient Eastern and Western audiences – and the promoters of the tale – its tremendously wide currency in ancient and medieval cultures and its frequent literary use give it a place here. This is how it is told by Chaucer.

ONCE UPON A time there was a nobleman called Walter who was both good and powerful, much beloved by his people. After a time, when he had not married, they sent a deputation to him, saying, 'Marquis, please marry a wife so that we may have your son to take your place when you are gone from us.' And he replied: 'I shall marry when I find one whom I can love, and find suitable.' So they had to be content.

Now, there was a poor man, living humbly with his daughter, Griselda, near a well of fresh water. Walter was riding by, when he saw the girl, tall and beautiful, carrying a pot of water on her head. He asked her for a drink, and then noticing that she was lovelier than any woman he had ever seen, wished to marry her. In her one simple smock, and barefoot, she arrived at the castle. Women attendants bathed her, dressed her in fine clothes, and prepared her for marriage to their noble lord. After the extravagant wedding and great rejoicing of the people, Walter took Griselda into a private room and said: 'Now, wife, you must obey me in all that I wish, and respect my thoughts and commands whatever they may be.' So she promised that she would, and for a while they were very happy indeed.

In a year's time a daughter was born to them, a very beautiful child, as fair as her mother. Now came the first great test of Griselda's married life. Her husband came to her and said, 'The people who love me are dissatisfied with you. They say that I should not have married someone in such a low station of life as yourself. They do not wish me to have children by you, so the child must be taken away and killed.' Griselda was stricken to the heart, but she knew she must do everything her husband required, so she agreed to have the child taken away to be killed in a remote spot. As the huntsman came in to drag the little girl from her arms, she held her for just a moment, and said calmly to him: 'Do bury her deep in the earth when it is done, that she will not be torn by wild beasts.' Then she kissed her daughter, and sat silently for a while. Not for a moment did she think ill of her husband, or cry out in her pain. Her life with Walter continued as before, with but one difference, that she never mentioned her daughter's name.

Another year passed, and a son of great beauty was born to Griselda. The loss of the other child seemed to have faded from her mind as Griselda cradled her son in her arms, singing to him softly as she fed him. Walter appeared to be satisfied with her, and it seemed that all was well with their life together. But, when the boy was two years old, Griselda had a severe test of her love for her husband. He once more said to her, 'Wife, the people are very distressed in case the grandson of a peasant like your father should inherit my land, and rule them. They demand that he, too, be taken from you and killed. It is my will that this should be done,' and he left her without another word.

Patient Griselda held the child for the last time, and kissed it. Then she said to the same huntsman who had taken away her daughter, 'Bury the body deep in the earth, where no beasts or birds of prey can reach him.' And without so much as a tear she handed over the infant, wrapped in his warmest clothes against the morning's chill. After that day she did not speak of the baby, yet she treated her husband with the same tenderness and respect as always. She ran the great house with perfect calm and dignity, as if indeed she had been a true noblewoman instead of a poor peasant's daughter, brought up in poverty.

Now, in reality, Walter was not guilty of his children's murder, but had despatched them to his sister's country estate, there to be brought up in luxury and kindness by her. He thought to test Griselda, hoping to find in her character some flaw, some chink in that armour of calm, that goodness of spirit and heart which he could scarcely believe was true and real.

'For,' he thought, 'she cannot be as good and as true as she appears, devoted to me even after these apparently savage acts of mine. Yet, I will test her further.'

So, he said to her, 'Griselda, I have some news for you which I must tell you now. For some time past, my life has not been happy, and my love for you has died.

My marriage to you was obviously a great mistake, no one was pleased with my marrying a girl of such low degree. My friends will not receive me because of this, and I have now sent for an annulment. You must stop wearing the clothes which should grace a wife of mine, and return to wearing the smock in which you came here. Soon the noble lady whom I am to marry will be coming. Please get the castle in order for her to take over, see to it that everything is replenished and fresh for her. Do you understand what I have said?' he asked, for she did not even change her expression of calm serenity as he was speaking.

'Yes, my lord,' said Griselda, smoothing the fine dress she was wearing with her slim hands, 'I understand. All will be done as you desire. Just let me remove these fineries and I will take the cleaning of the rooms as my own personal responsibility. I wish you every good fortune in your new happiness.' And she went away to remove her clothes.

She had preserved in her chest the plain simple smock in which she had arrived, this she took out and put on. Her jewels, furs, silks and fine shoes she returned to Walter, and took up her task as housekeeper with much enthusiasm. What went on in her mind and heart no one knew. It did not appear to her that she was badly done by at all, for she just thought she was making good her promise to Walter when he married her, that she would carry out without question everything required of her.

She visited her father in his simple house, and spent a day with him, telling him what had happened. 'You must return here,' he cried, 'I may be a peasant, but you are my beloved daughter, and I will look after you as I did before. I always knew that this would happen, it is not natural that one so highborn as he should take one such as we are for his wife.'

'I will have to go back and prepare everything for the wedding feast,' said Griselda, with simple dignity, 'I have been asked to attend to it, and attend to it I shall. Afterwards, when they are married, I will come back home.' So she went back to the castle, walking strongly away in her bare feet, the white smock her only garment.

Now, the noble Walter had sent a letter to his sister, asking her to send with all speed, dressed in fine clothes and jewels, his daughter. The girl was like a princess, tall and fair, and was most excited about the journey upon which she was going, in her aunt's wonderful coach and six horses, but she knew not why. Her younger brother, now a handsome stripling, as good looking as his father had been at the time of the marriage to Griselda, came too. They both were brought swiftly to the castle, and led to the guest chambers.

Griselda was waiting at the door, with fresh flowers for the supposed bride, and gave them to her with charming grace. Walter called Griselda to him and asked: 'Is she not beautiful, my new bride?' and Griselda answered: 'Yes, my lord, she is fair. But, and this is the only thing I would like to say to you – I pray you treat this young Princess with greater care than you did me, for as she is so delicate and gently-born, she might not be able to bear what I have done unquestioningly and faithfully, and her heart might break.' Then she went away to prepare the wedding feast with the other servants.

The whole castle was decorated with flowers and ribbons; flags and fine carpets were hung from the balconies. Music and singing came from the minstrels' gallery. People arrived from every part of Walter's dominions to do him honour at his wedding. Still patient Griselda attended to every detail, waiting upon the lady and her young brother herself, seeing that everything was to their liking. The nobleman called Griselda to him and said, 'Look, does she not have every feature as you once had when you were young, and my wife? Will you not consider her a suitable wife for me, as my people do, and wish her every good fortune?' He looked at her very strangely, waiting to hear her reply.

'Yes, my lord,' she answered, 'she is indeed very fair, and young, and I wish you all joy with each other.'

Her eyes were raised to his, and in them he read all that was true, faithful, and honest. His heart smote him, and he seized her hands in his, pulling himself to his feet. 'Dearest Griselda!' he cried. 'Forgive me, for I have tested you cruelly, but I had to know if you really loved me enough to suffer all these things for my sake. Know, sweet and faithful wife, that this Princess whom I have brought here and her brother are none other than our own dear children, whom you believed dead. Come, let me place this fur robe upon you, and I pray you will take your seat here beside me at the table, so that you will for the rest of our lives be my own beloved wife.'

Then at last did Griselda's tears fall, and she wept as she embraced her long-lost daughter and her handsome son, and thanked God that they were returned to her. She swooned twice, and each time her husband raised her up with loving hands.

And Walter, his misgivings about her dispelled, did everything in his power to make her forget the dreadful years of her testing. They lived devoted to each other, and to their children, for the rest of their days, as happy as true and faithful lovers can. Griselda's father, after he understood the tale they told him, was brought to the castle, and he, too, lived the rest of his life in comfort and tranquillity, free of all care.

How Evil Produces Evil

In the form of 'The Pardoner's Tale', this allegory is firmly rooted at the very base of English literature, through Geoffrey Chaucer's The Canterbury Tales *of nearly six centuries ago. In the records of its transmission through several cultures, however, it enables us to study the preoccupations of each people employing it. In the ancient Indian form, it is presented to inculcate a moral; in its Arabian garb (and the Italian) the chief figure is Jesus, where the religious aspect is stressed. The old German version is anti-Jewish, and the Florentine recension favours the wisdom of a hermit. The Central Asian writing was by the 13th-century major Sufi mystic – of Chaucerian rank in Persian – Fariduddin Attar; and here the application is that of the gnostic, to the effect that there is an unperceived world beyond normal perceptions. The following version is from the 16th-century Italian; the story is famous, too, as the plot of Hans Sachs' 1547 Meisterlied.*

A CERTAIN HERMIT was walking one day in a deserted place, when he came across an enormous cave, the entrance to which was not easily visible. He decided to rest inside, and entered. Soon, however, he noticed the bright reflection of the light upon a large quantity of gold within.

The hermit, as soon as he became aware of what he had seen, took to his heels and fled as fast as he could.

Now in this desert area were three robbers, who spent much time there so that they could steal from travellers. Before long the pious man blundered into them. The thieves were surprised, and even alarmed, at the sight of a man running, with nothing in pursuit; but they came out of their ambush and stopped him, asking him what was the matter.

'I am fleeing, brothers,' he said, 'from the Devil, who is racing after me.'

Now the bandits could not see anything following the devout old man, and they said, 'Show us what is after you.'

'I will,' he said (for he was afraid of them) and led them to the cave, at the same time begging them not to go near it. By this time, of course, the thieves were greatly interested, and insisted that they should be shown whatever it was that had caused such alarm.

'Here,' he said, 'is death, which was running after me.'

The villains were, of course, delighted. They

naturally regarded the recluse as somewhat touched, and sent him on his way, while they revelled in their good fortune.

Now the thieves began to discuss what they should do with the booty; for they were afraid of leaving it alone again. Finally they decided that one of their number should take a little gold to the city and with it buy food and other necessities, and then they would proceed to the division of the spoils.

One of the ruffians volunteered to run the errand. He thought to himself: 'When I am in town I can eat all I wish. Then I can poison the rest of the food, so that it kills the other two, and all the treasure will be mine.'

While the rogue was away, however, his companions were also thinking. They decided that as soon as he returned, they would kill him, eat the food, and divide the spoils so as to gain the additional third share that would otherwise be his.

The moment the first thief arrived back at the cave with the provisions, the two others fell upon him and stabbed him to death. Then they ate all the food, and expired of the poison which their friend had bought and put into it. So the gold, after all, did indeed spell death, as the hermit predicted, for whoever was influenced by it. And the treasure remained where it had been, in the cave, for a very long time.

The Ghoul and the Youth of Ispahan

Episodes from the English 'Jack the Giant-Killer' are found in favourite folktales about encounters with ogres all over the world. In 'Jack', the Giant roars 'Fee, fi, fo, fum!' or 'Fe, fa, fum!' And, in the Indian version, the Rakshasas say: 'Fee, faw, fum!' The Albanian variant of this story is very close to that of the Norse lad and the Troll; and the Sicilian 'Brave Shoemaker and the Giant' is almost identical. Several incidents from the Grimm's 'The Brave Little Tailor' appear in this cycle of stories. It is known in South America, where the Chilean adaptation is that of Don Juan Bolondron.

The following is the Persian recital, given by the Shah's personal story-teller to Sir John Malcolm. Parts of it may also be found in the Sanskrit Seventy Tales of a Parrot, *in the Nordic* Edda of Snorro, *and varieties have been noted in Cornwall and Kashmir.*

ONCE UPON A time there was a clever young lad of the ancient city of Ispahan, in Persia. He was out one day when he came upon a Ghoul, a sort of ogre-giant, terrible in size and horrible in temper. 'What can I do?' he asked himself. And well might he ask, for Ghouls love to enslave and destroy people, and even eat them up. All that the young man – Amin the True was his name – had with him was an egg and a lump of salt, both in his pocket.

Now, as everyone knows, the best form of defence is attack, so Amin approached the Ghoul, which was looking at him with frightful fury, and said:

'Ho! Ghoul – let's have a contest of strength.'

For a moment the Ghoul was puzzled, because human beings never spoke like that to him, and, like all Ghouls, he was not brilliantly intelligent. Then he said:

'You don't look very strong to me.'

'I may not look strong,' said Amin, 'but have you not heard that appearances can be deceptive? Here is a proof of my tremendous strength.'

He picked up a stone. 'Now I challenge you to squeeze water out of this.'

The Ghoul took the stone and tried. Then he said:

'No, it is impossible.'

'Not at all – it is easy,' replied Amin. While the Ghoul had been squeezing, Amin had placed the egg in his own hand. Now he took the stone in the same hand and squeezed.

There was a crushing sound as the egg broke and the Ghoul saw what he thought to be the liquid from the stone running between Amin's fingers: and all this was done without Amin showing any sign of strain at all.

Luckily it was not completely light, so the details of what was happening were not entirely visible to the monster.

Then Amin took up another stone and said:

'There is salt in this one, just crumble it between your fingers.'

The Ghoul looked at the stone, and saw that it was quite beyond his power to crush it, and he admitted that he could not.

'Oh, give it to me,' said Amin. He took it into the hand in which he had already hidden the lump of salt, and crumbled the salt into the hand of the amazed Ghoul.

'Now,' said the giant, 'you must stay the night with me,' and Amin agreed, for he guessed that he would always be able to get the better of him.

When they arrived at the immense cavern which was his host's home, the Ghoul threw Amin an enormous bag made from the hides of no less than six oxen, and said:

'Go and fill this with water, while I make the fire ready to cook.'

He went away in search of wood.

Amin wondered what he could do about the water, and then an idea occurred to him. He could hardly drag the bag more than a few feet, so he abandoned it and went down to the stream and started to dig a small channel.

Soon the Ghoul appeared and cried:

'Why are you taking so long? Can't you lift a little bag of water?'

'No, my friend,' said Amin, 'since you are being so hospitable to me, I have decided to dig a channel to bring the water to you, so that you always have a supply – see, I have started already. There is no point in feats of strength for their own sake; that is just a waste of time and effort.'

The Ghoul was hungry, so he said:

'Leave the water; I shall carry it.' And he picked up the bag as if it had been a feather and filled it at the river.

'Finish the channel tomorrow, if you want to,' he said.

The Ghoul ate a huge meal, and, in the darkness of the cave, Amin pretended to eat as well. Then the Ghoul pointed to a sleeping-place, and told Amin to lie down on it for the night.

But there was a crafty look in the Ghoul's eyes, and Amin placed a large pillow in the place where he should be sleeping and hid himself in a corner.

A little before daybreak, the Ghoul woke up. Seizing an immense tree-trunk, he smashed it down on Amin's bed. There was not even a groan, and the Ghoul grinned as he thought that he must have crushed Amin to pulp. Just to make sure, he pounded the bed seven times.

Now the Ghoul went back to sleep, but he had hardly settled himself again when Amin, who had crept back into his own bed, cried out:

'Friend Ghoul, what insect could that be which disturbed me by its flapping? I counted the beat of its wings seven times. Although such things cannot hurt men, they can be disturbing to someone who is sleeping.'

The Ghoul was aroused to such heights of fear at hearing that this was a man who felt a shattering blow, seven blows, only as the wings of an insect, that he fled headlong from his cave, leaving Amin its master.

Amin took up a gun which had been left by some victim of the Ghoul, and went out to scout. He had not gone very far when he saw the Ghoul coming back. In his hand he held a large club, and beside him was a fox.

Amin realised that the cunning fox had explained matters to the Ghoul; but he was equal to the challenge. Aiming the gun, he shot it through the head.

'Take that!' he shouted, 'for disobedience.' To the

Ghoul he said:

'That liar,' pointing to the fox, 'had promised to bring me seven Ghouls, so that I might put them in chains and lead them back to the city of Ispahan: but he brought only you, who are already my slave!'

No sooner were the words out of his mouth than the Ghoul took to his heels. Using the club to help him, he leapt over rocks and precipices, and he was soon far out of sight.

The Pilgrim from Paradise

The theme of the crafty adventurer is common to a whole genre of stories; just as the entertainment possibilities in misunderstandings and the working of simpletons' minds are two further well-exploited themes, especially in folklore. These elements are combined in a humorous whole in a tale which is a favourite – and has been such for centuries – in countries as far apart as Norway, Brittany, Italy and Southern India. A distinctive characteristic of this story is that, from the frozen North to the sunbaked South-East of Asia, the essential incidents remain remarkably similar. This version is from the nineteenth-century Bombay collection of Pandit Natesa Sastri.

A KINDLY AND charitable, somewhat simple woman, married to a rich miser, once lived in a village where a certain rogue had made up his mind to fool the woman when he could find an opportunity. One day this man saw the miser ride out to make a tour of his land, and decided that the time to work his trick had arrived. He made his way to the house where the couple lived, and threw himself upon the ground, as if completely exhausted.

The good woman came out at once, asking what his trouble was, and where he was from. 'I am a traveller from paradise,' he said, 'and I have been sent by an ancient couple, to seek news of their son and his wife.'

The lady was very much impressed that she had a visitor from the mysterious, inaccessible Mount Kailasa of the Himalayas, and wondered aloud who these lucky people could be whom her guest represented.

The villain gave the names of her husband's parents, whom he knew to be dead, and this of course only increased her interest. 'And how are they?' she asked. 'Are they well? If only my husband were at home, to hear your news of his dear old father and mother.' She asked him to sit down to rest, and plied him with question after question about the departed ones.

She played into the swindler's very hands by asking

him whether her parents-in-law had enough to wear and to eat, and if they were really happy.

The thief was anxious to be on his way before the miser returned, so he made short work of his answers. 'Lady,' he said, 'I have no words to describe their miserable state. In the world beyond they have no clothes, no food, only some water to drink. How lucky that you cannot see their sufferings.'

'But why should it be so with them,' she asked, 'when their son has so much, and when I have everything I need?'

To cut a long story short, she went into the house and brought out a large quantity of clothes and all her own jewels. 'Clothes and jewels will not help their hunger,' said the confidence man: and the trusting woman went back into the house and brought as much of her husband's money as she could find. Collecting up his loot, the villain made off as fast as he could.

Not long afterwards the husband returned, and you can imagine his rage when he heard from the excited lady how a messenger from paradise had brought grave news and taken succour to his mother and father. But there was no time to be lost. Choking back his fury, he merely asked her which way the messenger had gone, and he spurred his horse in hot pursuit.

Before long the miser saw the thief, and started to

gain on him minute by minute. The deceiver, realising that he could not escape, decided to rely on his wits, and climbed up a tall tree with his bundle of booty.

As soon as the miser arrived at the bottom of the tree, he called upon the thief to come down. 'Sorry,' said the swindler, 'I am making my way heavenwards, to Kailasa.' He climbed to the very top of the towering peepul tree.

The miser settled himself to wait; but then he became impatient, and started laboriously to climb up after the thief. Waiting until he had almost reached him, the agile thief threw down all the things he had with him and shinned down the tree faster than the miser could follow. Leaping upon the miser's horse, he rode it into the thickest part of the jungle he could find.

The miser, of course, was now completely outwitted. Sorrowfully, he made his limping way back to his home. There was his wife, with radiant face, who called out to him in delight: 'Ah, so you have even handed over your horse to be taken to paradise, so that your dear old father can ride.'

Unable to admit that he was as much a fool as she had been, the miser could only try to cover his rage and folly by saying: 'Yes, that's right…'

The Blind Ones and the Matter of the Elephant

Reading the controversies of folklore scholars sometimes feels more like being on a battlefield than strolling in the groves of academe. Edward Clodd (1840–1930), President of the British Folk-Lore Society, insisted that folk traditions represented the 'persistence of barbaric elements' until the present day. 'Rumpelstiltskin' was an example of a primitive name-taboo, found in East Anglia (as 'Tom Tit Tot') quite recently, and so on. Rabbi Moses Gaster of Romania (1856–1934), another President of the same Society, insisted, on the other hand, that tales were 'the last and modern development of folk-lore'. Were these the only possible positions? No. According to a third President of the Folk-Lore Society, Alfred Nutt (1856–1912), 'sometimes it is and sometimes it isn't':

'On the sea shore we may pick up fossils… reaching back into a past incalculably remote… we may also pick up worn

and rounded fragments of ginger beer bottles flung away perhaps only six months before.'

It all puts one in mind of an anecdote of the Eastern folklore figure Mulla Nasrudin:

Nasrudin entered the Mosque and said to the people: 'Do you know what I am going to tell you?' There were shouts of 'No'; so he said: 'Then I shall not bother with such ignoramuses.' The following day he asked the same question again, from the pulpit. The answer was 'Yes'. 'Then I don't need to tell you!' he said and went out. The third time, when he repeated his question, the people cried: 'Some of us do, some of us do not!' Nasrudin said: 'Then let those who do tell those who do not know!' And he left the building.

The following story, of the unity of all knowledge, from the great 13th century mystic of Balkh (now Afghanistan), Maulana Jalaluddin Rumi, may perhaps get to the heart of the problem.

Beyond Ghor there was a city. All its inhabitants were blind. A king with his entourage arrived nearby; he brought his army and camped in the desert. He had a mighty elephant, which he used in attack and to increase the people's awe.

The populace became anxious to see the elephant, and some sightless ones from among this blind community ran like fools to find it.

As they did not even know the form or shape of the elephant they groped sightlessly, gathering information by touching some part of it.

Each thought that he knew something, because he could feel a part.

When they returned to their fellow-citizens, eager groups clustered around them. Each of these was anxious, misguidedly, to learn the truth from those who were themselves astray.

They asked about the form, the shape of the elephant, and they listened to all that they were told.

The man whose hand had reached an ear was asked about the elephant's nature. He said: 'It is a large, rough thing, wide and broad, like a rug.'

And the one who had felt the trunk said: 'I have the real facts about it. It is like a straight and hollow pipe, awful and destructive.'

The one who had felt its feet and legs said:

'It is mighty and firm, like a pillar.'

Each had felt one part out of many. Each had

perceived it wrongly. No mind knew all: knowledge is not the companion of the blind. All imagined something, something incorrect.

The created is not informed about divinity. There is no Way in this science by means of the ordinary intellect.

Anpu and Bata

The tale of Anpu and Bata, found in an Ancient Egyptian papyrus manuscript, is more than three thousand years old, and is regarded as the oldest story that has come down to us in writing. It may well have been an ancient tradition even then. One of the most interesting things about it is that elements found in tales all over the world ever since are contained in it. The first part has a parallel in the Biblical story of Joseph and the Wife of Potiphar. The core of the story – the life-token indicating death and the 'separable soul' – occurs in over eight hundred versions in Europe alone, and the reciters are unlikely to know that they are part of a line of transmission from the Nineteenth Dynasty of Pharaonic Egypt.

The story is sometimes found, conflated with all or much of the Perseus and Andromeda myth, associated with the exploits of a dragon-slayer, which is encountered in almost every country in the world.

The crumbling papyrus roll, in the British Museum,

contains a message from the original scribe, a threat to those who might abuse it, which is similar to those found on Eastern manuscripts even today:

'Excellently finished in peace for the Ka of the scribe of the Treasury Kagabu, of the Treasury of Pharaoh. And for the Scribe Hora, and the Scribe Meramapt. Written by the Scribe Anena, the owner of this roll. He who speaks against this scroll, may Tahuti smite him!'

It was the custom of Eastern kings, when pleased with a story related to them, to order it to be written down and placed in the treasury.

Once there lived in Egypt two brothers, and they loved each other greatly. The elder had a beautiful young wife, and a fine pair of oxen for the fields. His name was Anpu, and his younger brother's name was Bata. This young man did everything for his brother, followed him and the oxen to the fields, waited upon him like a servant, harvested the corn, tended the animals. He worked for him day and night; for his brother, in his eyes, had no equal in all the land of Egypt.

Now when the time for ploughing the land arrived, the elder brother said to Bata, 'Come with the seeds tomorrow early to the fields, for we must begin sowing, because the Nile flood has retreated from the earth and the day is propitious.'

Anpu having gone on ahead, it was left for Bata to bring the seed, so he went to the door of the house, and said to his sister-in-law, Anpu's beautiful young wife, 'Let me have the corn from the bin, for my brother and I need it today.' The woman replied, 'Come in and get it yourself, for I am busy doing my hair and I cannot drop my pins and ribbons and get the corn.' So he went in, and helped himself to as much corn as he could carry, for he wanted to start the day of planting well, as the day was propitious.

Seeing him carrying such a load, the wife of his brother said, 'You are strong and good-looking, indeed. I had not noticed that you were so presentable before. Come, stay with me a little while here before you go to the fields, for you will both be away all day, and I shall be lonely. Give me something to remember when I am alone.'

Bata recoiled at the woman's words, and his face darkened with rage. He said, 'You are like a mother to me, for are you not my respected brother's wife? I will forget what you have just spoken. Do you forget it, also.' And he went away to the fields, trying to erase her suggestion from his mind, for she was his brother's wife, and though beautiful, now appeared evil in his eyes.

All day they laboured in the fields, and at evening Anpu and Bata returned home. They expected to find food ready as usual, when they came to the house. But there was no fire, no light, no smell of cooking.

Bata went to the stable to attend to the animals, and Anpu went in to see what was the matter with his wife. She was lying huddled under the quilt, crying as if she were in pain.

'What is the matter with you?' he asked. 'Has anyone been here in my absence to upset you like this?'

'The only one here in your absence was your wretched brother!' she cried. 'Ask him what is the matter with me!'

'But what are you saying? Has he laid hands upon you?' shouted the enraged husband.

'Yes,' she replied, 'I was here doing my hair when

he came in for the seeds, and he said to me "Be with me a while before I go to the fields and my brother will never know" and he violated me. Oh, I cannot look at you for shame, my husband!'

So Anpu sharpened his knife, and stood outside the stable ready to kill his brother as soon as he came to join him for the evening meal.

All unaware of this, the younger brother went about his tasks in the stable, when suddenly his favourite cow spoke to him:

'Beware, Bata, your brother has sharpened his knife and is waiting to kill you behind the door. Run, do not go back to the house, or you will die.'

The young man looked out of the stable and saw his brother standing strangely still, with his knife in his hand. Fearing that he could never explain the true state of affairs to his brother, he made a hole in the mud wall of the barn and fled as fast as his feet would carry him. But the elder brother heard him running, and chased after him. The light of murder was in his eyes.

So, in great fear, Bata called out: 'Oh Great Ra Harakhiti, Mighty Lord, You are He who divides the Evil from the Good! Save me!' and Ra answered his prayer.

A mighty river sprang up between the two brothers, a river that Anpu could not cross, even if he had had a boat, for it was full of crocodiles. The elder brother was furious that he could not reach Bata to kill him, and cursed him from the other bank.

But Bata called out in a loud voice to him: 'O my brother, do not think ill of me. I cannot prove to you that I did nothing wrong, but my cow warned me, and I fled from you in fear. Why did you come to kill me before you asked me if I had done what you believed I did?'

And his brother said: 'Tell me yourself, then, what truly happened?'

Bata answered, 'I went to the bin to get the seed myself, for your wife told me she was doing her hair and did not wish to leave her toilette to attend to me. Then, after I had helped myself, she said I looked strong and handsome, and tempted me to stay with her for a short while, saying that you would not know. You see how the truth has been changed.'

'Will you swear the oath by Ra Harakhiti that what you have said is true?' cried the elder brother.

'By Ra Harakhiti I swear that it is true,' said the younger brother, and he took his knife, and cut a piece of his flesh, and threw it into the water, and the crocodiles ate it. Then the elder brother was satisfied, and he wept for Bata and cursed his wife. He knew that he could not reach his brother, because of the crocodiles, and he stood there, putting away his knife.

'Now we know that you have done a bad thing, trying to kill me, will you now do a good thing for me?' said Bata.

Anpu said he would, so his brother told him, 'I am going away to the valley of the acacia. So you go to your house, and look to your cattle. Now this is what you can do for me; my soul shall be drawn out, and put into the flower of the acacia. When the acacia is cut down, as it will be, put the flower in a glass of cold water, for my soul shall be in it. When someone gives you a glass of beer in your hand, and it is agitating in the glass, then do not stay, but go and find the flower, even if you search for seven years, and put it in the water. Farewell.'

Then the youth stopped speaking these strange things, and went to the valley of the acacia.

His brother turned away and went back to his house, and he was angered against his wife, so he killed her in the heat of his wrath.

Then he threw his knife away, and looked after his cattle and his fields himself, sorrowing for his brother.

A long time after this had happened, the younger brother was living in the valley of the acacia. He had drawn out his soul, and it lived in the topmost flower of the acacia tree. He had built himself a small house in which he lived, and it was full of good things.

One day, walking in the valley, he met the Nine Gods, who were going forth to look upon the whole land of Egypt. The Nine Gods were talking with each other when Bata came upon them, and they said to him, 'O Bata, Bull of the Nine Gods, why are you walking alone? Your brother has slain his wife, and all is level between you. His transgression is forgiven.'

Then, as Bata knelt before them, Ra Harakhiti said to Khnumu, 'So that he will not be forever alone, make a woman for Bata, a mate for his loneliness.' And Khnumu made a wife for him. She was more beautiful than any woman had ever been before. The seven Hathors came to see her when she was created, and they said of one accord: 'She will die a sharp death, though the essence of every god is in her!'

All the day Bata hunted and in the evening he came back and placed all his spoils at his wife's feet, for he loved her very much. He said to her one day, 'Now, I must warn you, never go too near the sea, for if it should seize you, and want to carry you away, I cannot save you, for my soul is in the flower at the top of the acacia, and I have no power, other than in that flower.'

When she heard his secret she smiled, and thought about it much.

Next day she went to walk beside the sea, and the sea saw her, and began to cast its waves up towards her. She took to her heels and, being frightened by the passion of the sea, ran away from it. She entered her house, and the sea called to the acacia: 'I want to have that woman, I wish that I could take her!' Then the acacia brought a curl from her hair which the woman had cut off while sitting under the tree, and dropped it into the water. The sea carried it to the place where the fullers washed the clothes of the Pharaoh.

One of the washermen who was standing on the sand picked up the curl of hair, and it smelt so sweet that it almost took his senses away. He put it into the clothing which was being taken to the Pharaoh, and when Pharaoh smelt it he was enraptured.

'Where did this rare and wonderful scent come from?' cried Pharaoh. 'Bring the wise men, so that they too may smell it and tell me.'

The wise men came, with their signs and portents, and told the Pharaoh, 'The scent comes from the curl from the hair of a daughter of Ra Harakhiti; the essence of every god is in her. Send messengers to the borders of the sea, and in the valley of the acacia she will be found.'

So the Pharaoh sent many men to the valley of the acacia, and they tried to take the wife of Bata, but he killed them all. None of these men returned to the Pharaoh, and so he sent more, this time men on horseback and strong soldiers, to bring her to him.

Bata had to let her go, but they did not kill him. He remained behind, under the acacia, feeling very distressed. Somehow, from his mind he tried to send a message to his brother, reminding him of what he had said to Anpu across the river of the crocodiles, the last time that he had seen him.

The beautiful woman pleased the Pharaoh very much, and he gave her everything in his power.

'Pharaoh,' said she, after he had presented her with gold and jewels and rarest rings, 'send men to cut down the acacia, for my husband's soul is in the topmost flower, and I would that he were dead.' So the men went and chopped the tree in the valley so that the topmost flower, in which was the soul of Bata, fell to the ground, and he, too, fell dead.

At that very moment, someone handed Anpu, the elder brother, a glass of beer, and the liquid became agitated as he was about to drink it. He remembered what his brother had told him, all that long time ago. He got his stick and his sandals, his clothes for travelling, and set off.

He travelled all day and all night, and arrived at the valley of the acacia. Then he saw that the tree had been cut down, and saw the body of his brother lying dead. He wept bitterly, and looked everywhere for the flower which contained the soul of his brother. But he could not find it. He lay down to sleep under the tree, and said to himself – 'Tomorrow, and tomorrow, and tomorrow I will seek it; for I will spend all the days of my life, if necessary, to find the flower.'

Next day he did not find it, but he discovered, in a crack in the earth, a seed. He put the seed in a glass of water, and it sprouted. It was soon the flower containing his brother's soul. Within a few minutes the body of Bata shuddered under the cloth which covered it, and soon he was standing well and strong before Anpu. They embraced each other joyfully, and sat talking together for many hours.

Then Bata said to his brother, 'I am to become a great bull, by favour of the gods, and you are to get on my back. By the time the sun has risen thrice I shall be in the place where my wife makes a fool of the Pharaoh. And, when I am before the Pharaoh, you shall be taken to him, and he will give you gold and silver, and good things in return. I will be thought of by all as a great marvel, and you will return to our old village home a rich man.' Before Anpu's eyes he turned into a huge bull. So, the elder brother got onto his back, and within three days they were before the Pharaoh.

The Pharaoh had never before seen such a fine creature, in all dominions of the Upper and the Lower Nile, so he gave many presents to the elder brother, and took Bata in his bull form to the royal stables to be looked after in great style. The gigantic bull was so tame that it was often garlanded with flowers by the royal ladies. One day when his wife, now a Princess by command of the Pharaoh, came near to him, the bull said in his human voice, 'I am alive, and now the gods have in their wisdom, caused me to be in this marvellous bull's body.'

She was greatly affrighted, and wondered how she

could get rid of her husband yet again. So she went to the Pharaoh and said, 'My lord, I will never be happy unless I have for my illness the liver of that creature, which I am sure is fit for nothing else but to be eaten!' So at once the Pharaoh gave orders for the animal to be slaughtered, and said, 'Let the liver be given to the Princess, so that she will soon be well again.'

A tremendous feast was planned, and the bull was to be sacrificed to the gods. As he was being slaughtered, the bull shook two drops of blood from his shoulder wound onto the walls of the royal palace. The blood dripped from each side of the gigantic door, and where the blood soaked into the ground two Persea trees grew. They grew and grew, each day taller, and each of them was perfect in every way.

A courtier went to tell the Pharaoh, 'Lo, there are two giant trees growing, one on each side of the great door of the palace, these are propitious signs, oh Pharaoh!' And there was much rejoicing because of these trees, and many people made offerings to them, because of their miraculous growth from the bull's blood.

The ladies of the court went out, and placed garlands of flowers around the trees, and prayed to them.

When his wife came, Bata said to her from the trees, in his own voice, which she knew so well, 'Deceitful woman, I am Bata, who you have thrice betrayed. First you went to the Pharaoh, then you had my soul-tree cut down, then you had the ox slain. Now I am in the strength of these trees. I shall never die!'

So the Princess went to the Pharaoh and said, 'As you love me, will you do me a small favour? I do not like the sight of those two grotesque Persea trees, one on each side of the great door of the palace. Do you please give orders that they be cut down, for they grow even uglier every day, and one day they will bring the palace down, I am sure!'

The Pharaoh, besotted with his love for her, consented, and the next day woodcutters were chopping with might and main at the beautiful Persea trees. The Princess was standing not far away, looking at this activity, rejoicing in her heart, when a tiny chip of wood flew into her mouth. She was so startled that she swallowed it. The trees were at that moment completely cut down, and fell outside the Palace gates.

When nine months had passed, a son was born to the Princess, and there was rejoicing all through the land, for the Pharaoh thought that the child was his son. As the months went by, the Pharaoh loved the baby even more, and raised him to be the royal son of Kush, heir of all the lands of the Upper and Lower Nile.

Not many days after that, the Pharaoh died.

Then the Prince, the heir of the lands, said:

'Let all my nobles come before me, that I may tell them all that has happened to me.'

They came, and he told them everything. His elder brother was brought from the village, to be made a minister at his court. Then they brought his wife, and they judged her and she received her punishment.

He was thirty years King of Egypt, and so endeared himself to the people that his brother took his place when he died.

God is Stronger

A Hebrew hymn relating to the Holy Land (beginning 'A kid, a kid my father bought') is closely similar to the English rhymed tale, 'The House that Jack Built'. Varieties of this cumulative tale are found in Norse and in Punjabi, and in Sri Lanka; similar stories have been noted in Scotland and Kashmir. This is the version found in traditional Malagasy folklore, recorded in Madagascar (Malagasy Republic).

IBOTITY HAD CLIMBED a tree when the wind blew, the tree split, Ibotity fell, and his leg was broken. 'The tree is strong, for it broke my leg,' he said.

'It is the wind which is stronger than the tree,' said the tree.

But the wind said that the hill was stronger, since it could stop the wind. Ibotity, of course, thought that strength was of the hill, to be able to stop the wind, which split the tree, which broke his leg.

'No,' said the hill, explaining that the mouse was strong for it could burrow into the hill. But the mouse denied this: 'For I can be killed by the cat' – and so Ibotity thought that the cat must be strongest of all.

Not so; the cat explained that it could be caught by a rope, and Ibotity thought that this, then, must be the strongest thing.

The rope, however, explained that it could be cut by iron, which was therefore stronger. The iron, in its turn, denied being strongest, since it could be made soft by fire.

Ibotity now thought that the fire must be strongest, to soften the iron: which cut the rope, which bound the cat, which caught the mouse, which undermined the hill, which stopped the wind, which split the tree – which broke the leg of Ibotity.

The fire then said that water was stronger; and the water claimed that the canoe was yet stronger, for it cleft the water. But the canoe was overcome by the rock, and the rock by man, and man by the magician, and the magician by the ordeal by poison, and the ordeal by God, so God is the strongest of all:

'Then Ibotity knew that God could beat the ordeal, which stopped the magician, who overwhelms man, who breaks the rock, which overcomes the canoe, which cleaves the water, which puts out fire, which softens iron, which severs the rope, which binds the cat, which kills the mouse, which undermines the hill, which stops the wind, which splits the tree, which breaks the leg of Ibotity.'

The Happiest Man in the World

Although this tale is found in the story-books of both the East and West, it is far less often represented there than most traditional tales. Taoist and Sufi masters are reputed to have used it to illustrate the theme that 'the quest is what teaches you that only the end has meaning, not the assumption of what the end might be'.

This is the only story in this collection which seems to be increasing in currency, particularly in the oral transmission. When I was collecting tales in Europe, Asia and Africa a quarter of a century ago, I did not find a single example. Between 1960 and 1978, however, no fewer than ten story-tellers, in six different countries, provided versions.

The particular shape given here is a current one from Uzbekistan. The tale is more usually found as a two-liner, something like this:

'A man once heard that he would attain to wisdom if

he could meet the Happiest Man in the World, and obtain his shirt.

'It took him nearly all his life to find him. And then he noticed that the Happiest Man did not own a shirt.'

A MAN WHO was living in comfortable enough circumstances went one day to see a certain sage, reputed to have all knowledge. He said to him:

'Great Sage, I have no material problems, and yet I am always unsettled. For years I have tried to be happy, to find an answer to my inner thoughts, to come to terms with the world. Please advise me as to how I can be cured of this malaise.'

The sage answered:

'My friend, what is hidden to some is apparent to others. Again, what is apparent to some is hidden to others. I have the answer to your ailment, though it is no ordinary medication. You must set out on your travels, seeking the happiest man in the world. As soon as you find him, you must ask him for his shirt, and put it on.'

This seeker thereupon restlessly started looking for happy men. One after another he found them and questioned them. Again and again they said: 'Yes, I am happy, but there is one happier than me.'

After travelling through one country after another for many, many days, he found the wood in which everyone said lived the happiest man in the world.

He heard the sound of laughter coming from among the trees, and quickened his step until he came upon a man sitting in a glade.

'Are you the happiest man in the world, as people

say?' he asked.

'Certainly I am,' said the other man.

'My name is so-and-so, my condition is such-and-such, and my remedy, ordered by the greatest sage, is to wear your shirt. Please give it to me; I will give you anything I have in exchange.'

The happiest man looked at him closely, and he laughed. He laughed and he laughed and he laughed. When he had quietened down a little, the restless man, rather annoyed at this reaction, said:

'Are you unhinged, that you laugh at such a serious request?'

'Perhaps,' said the happiest man, 'but if you had only taken the trouble to look, you would have seen that I do not possess a shirt.'

'What, then am I to do now?'

'You will now be cured. Striving for something unattainable provides the exercise to achieve that which is needed: as when a man gathers all his strength to jump across a stream as if it were far wider than it is. He gets across the stream.'

The happiest man in the world then took off the turban whose end had concealed his face. The restless man saw that he was none other than the great sage who had originally advised him.

'But why did you not tell me all this years ago, when I came to see you?' the restless man asked in puzzlement.

'Because you were not ready then to understand. You needed certain experiences, and they had to be given to you in a manner which would ensure that you went through them.'

The Gorgon's Head

The Greek idea of the head of a Gorgon, one look at which can turn one into stone, is so arresting as never to be forgotten when once heard. The myth of the adventures of Perseus (told by Kingsley in The Heroes*) has all the elements of folktales: the magical apparatus; the perilous voyage; the beautiful maiden, daughter of a King; the threat of death, and the killing of a monster all figure prominently. The legend of St George has been seen as but a re-telling of the 'killing of the monster and rescue of the maiden' episodes from this narrative. According to early commentators, the theme is a portrayal of the victory of the Christian hero over evil, though later analysts saw it as a solar myth. More recently a psychoanalytical explanation has been preferred: and no doubt reinterpretations will continue, according to the opinions of the experts from time to time. Andrew Lang, the distinguished folklorist, reconstituted the myth in a fairy-tale book from Apollodorus, Simonides and Pindar as 'The Terrible Head', thus giving us an opportunity of comparing a version*

for popular consumption with the classical texts available in standard books.

This may represent the first stage of popularisation through which other literary presentations have gone in their transition into fireside telling.

ONCE UPON A time there was a King whose only child was a girl. Now the King had been very anxious to have a son, or at least a grandson, to come after him, but he was told by a prophet that his own daughter's son should kill him. This news terrified him so much that he determined never to let his daughter be married; for he thought it was better to have no grandson at all than to be killed by his grandson. He therefore called his workmen together, and bade them dig a deep round hole in the earth, and then he had a prison of brass built in the hole, and then, when it was finished, he locked up his daughter. No man ever saw her, and she never saw even the fields and the sea, but only the sky and the sun – for there was a wide open window in the roof of the house of brass. So the Princess would sit looking up at the sky, and watching the clouds float across, and wondering whether she should ever get out of her prison. Now one day it seemed to her that the sky opened above her and a great shower of shining gold fell through the window in the roof and lay glittering in her room. Not very long after, the Princess had a baby, a little boy, but when the King heard of it he was very angry and afraid, for now the child was born that should be his death. Yet, cowardly as he was, he had not quite the heart to kill the Princess and her baby outright, but he had them put in a huge brass-bound chest and thrust out to sea, so that they might either be drowned or starved, or perhaps come to a country where they would be out of his way.

So the Princess and the baby floated and drifted in the chest on the sea all day and all night, but the baby was not afraid of the waves nor of the wind; for he did not know that they could hurt him, and he slept quite soundly. And the Princess sang a song over him, and this was her song:

Child, my child, how sound you sleep!
Though your mother's care is deep
You can lie with heart at rest
In the narrow brass-bound chest;
In the starless night and drear
You can sleep, and never hear
Billows breaking, and the cry
Of the night-wind wandering by;
In soft purple mantle sleeping
With your little face on mine,
Hearing not your mother weeping
And the breaking of the brine.

Well, the daylight came at last, and the great chest was driven by the waves against the shore of an island. There it lay, with the Princess and her baby in it, till a man of that country came past, and saw it, and dragged it on to the beach, and when he had broken it open, behold! there was a beautiful lady and a little boy. So he took them home, and was very kind to them, and brought up the boy till he was a young man.

Now when the boy had come to his full strength, the King of that country fell in love with the mother and wanted to marry her; but he knew that she would never part from her boy. So he thought of a plan to get rid of the boy, and this was his plan.

A great Queen of a country not far off was going to be married, and this King said that all his subjects must bring him wedding presents to give her. And he made a feast to which he invited them all, and they all brought their presents; some brought gold cups, and some brought necklaces of gold and amber, and some brought beautiful horses. But the boy had nothing, though he was the son of a princess, for his mother had nothing to give him. Then the rest of the company began to laugh at him, and the King said: 'If you have nothing else to give, at least you might go and fetch the Terrible Head.'

The boy was proud and spoke without thinking:

'Then I swear that I *will* bring the Terrible Head, if it may be brought by a living man. But of what head you speak I know not.'

Then they told him that somewhere, a long way off, there dwelt three dreadful sisters, monstrous, ogrish women, with golden wings and claws of brass, and with serpents growing on their heads instead of hair. Now these women were so awful to look on that whoever saw them was at once turned into stone. And two of them could not be put to death, but the youngest, whose face was very beautiful, could be killed, and it was her head that the boy had promised to bring. You may imagine it was no easy adventure.

When he had heard all this he was pretty sorry that he had sworn to bring the Terrible Head, but he was determined to keep his oath. So he went out from the feast, where they all sat drinking and making merry; and he walked alone beside the sea in the dusk of the evening, at the place where the great chest, with himself and his mother in it, had been cast ashore.

There he went and sat down on a rock, looking towards the sea, and wondering how he should begin to fulfil his vow. Then he felt someone touch him on the shoulder; and he turned and saw a young man like a King's son, having with him a tall and beautiful lady, whose blue eyes shone like stars. They were taller than mortal men, and the young man had a staff in his hand with golden wings on it, and two golden serpents twisted around it, and he had wings on his cap and on his shoes. He spoke to the boy, and asked him why he was so unhappy; and the boy told him he had sworn to bring the Terrible Head, and knew not how to begin to set about the adventure.

Then the beautiful lady also spoke, and said that it was a foolish oath and hasty, but that it might be kept if a brave man had sworn it. Then the boy answered that he was not afraid, if only he knew the way.

Then the lady said that to kill the dreadful woman with the golden wings and the brass claws and to cut off her head, he needed three things: first a Cap of Darkness, which would make him invisible when he wore it; next, a Sword of Sharpness, which would cleave iron with one blow; and last, the Shoes of Swiftness, with which he might fly in the air.

The boy answered that he knew not where such things were to be procured, and that, lacking them, he could only try and fail. Then the young man, taking off his own shoes, said: 'First, you shall use these shoes till you have taken the Terrible Head, and then you must give them back to me. And with these shoes you will fly as fleet as a bird, or a thought, over the land and over the waves of the sea, wherever the shoes know the way. But there are ways which they do not know, roads beyond the borders of the world. And these roads must you travel. Now first, you must go to the Three Grey Sisters who live far off in the north, and are so very old that they have only one eye and one tooth among the three. You must creep up close to them and as one of them passes the eye to the other you must seize it, and refuse to give it up till they have told you the way to the Three Fairies of the Garden. They will give you the Cap of Darkness and the Sword of Sharpness, and show you how to wing beyond this world to the land of the

Terrible Head.'

Then the beautiful lady said, 'Go forth at once, and do not return to say goodbye to your mother, for these things must be done quickly, and the Shoes of Swiftness themselves will carry you to the land of the Three Grey Sisters – for they know the measure of that way.'

So the boy thanked her, and he fastened on the Shoes of Swiftness, and turned to say goodbye to the young man and the lady. But behold! they had vanished, he knew not how or where! Then he leaped in the air to try the Shoes of Swiftness and they carried him more swiftly than the wind, over the warm blue sea, over the happy lands of the south, over the northern peoples who drank mare's milk and lived in great waggons, wandering after their flocks. Across the wide rivers, where the wild fowl rose and fled before him, and over the plains and the cold North Sea he went, over the fields of snow and the hills of ice, to a place where the world ends, and all water is frozen and there are no men, nor beasts, nor any green grass.

There in a blue cave of the ice he found the Three Grey Sisters, the oldest of living things. Their hair was as white as snow, and their flesh of an icy blue, and they mumbled and nodded in a kind of dream, and their frozen breath hung around them like a cloud. Now the opening of the cave in the ice was narrow, and it was not easy to pass in without touching one of the Grey Sisters. But, floating on the Shoes of Swiftness, the boy just managed to steal in, and waited till one of the sisters said to another, who had their one eye:

'Sister, what do you see? Do you see old times coming back?'

'No, sister.'

'Then give me the eye, for perhaps I can see farther than you.'

Then the first sister passed the eye to the second, but as the second groped for it the boy took it cleverly out of her hand.

'Where is the eye, sister?' said the second grey woman.

'You have taken it yourself, sister,' said the first grey woman.

'Have you lost the eye, sister? Have you lost the eye?' said the third grey sister. 'Shall we never find it again, and see old times coming back?'

Then the boy slipped from behind them out of the cave into the air, and he laughed aloud.

When the old women heard that laugh they began to weep for now they knew that a stranger had robbed them, and that they could not help themselves. Their tears froze as they fell from the hollows where no eyes were, and rattled on the icy ground of the cave. Then they began to implore the boy to give them their eye back again, and he could not help feeling sorry for them, they were so pitiful. But he said he would never give them the eye till they told him the way to the Fairies of the Garden.

They wrung their hands miserably, for they guessed why he had come, and how he was going to try to win the Terrible Head. Now the Three Grey Sisters were akin to the Dreadful Women and it was hard for them to tell the boy the way. But at last they told him to keep always south, and with the land on his left and the sea on his right, till he reached the Island of the Fairies of the Garden. Then he gave them back the eye, and they began to look out once more for the old times coming back again. The boy flew south between sea and land, keeping the land always on his left hand, till he saw a beautiful island crowned with flowering trees. There he alighted, and there he found the Three Fairies of the Garden. They were like three very beautiful young women, dressed one in green, one in white and one in red, and they were singing and dancing around an apple tree with fruit of gold, and this was their song:

The Song of the Western Fairies

Round and round the apples of gold,
Round and round dance we;
Thus do we dance from the days of old
About the enchanted tree;

Round, and round, and round we go.
While the spring is green, or the stream shall flow,
Or the wind shall stir the sea!
There is none may taste of the golden fruit
Till the golden new times come;
Many a tree shall spring from shoot,
Many a blossom be withered at root,
Many a song be dumb;
Broken and still shall be many a lute
Or ever the new times come!
Round and round the tree of gold,
Round and round dance we,
So doth the great world spin from of old
Summer and winter, and fire and cold,
Song that is sung and tale that is told,
Even as we dance, that fold and unfold
Round the stem of the fairy tree!

These grave dancing fairies were very unlike the Grey Women, and they were glad to see the boy, and treated him kindly. Then they asked him why he had come; and he told them how he was sent to find the Sword of Sharpness and the Cap of Darkness. And the fairies gave him these, and a wallet, and a shield, and belted the sword, which had a diamond blade, around his waist, and the cap they set on his head, and told him that now even they could not see him, though they were fairies. Then he took it off, and they each kissed him and wished him good fortune, and then they began again their eternal dance around the golden tree, for it is their business to guard it till the new times come, or till the world's ending.

The boy put the cap on his head, and hung the wallet around his waist, and the shining shield on his shoulders, and he flew beyond the great river that lies coiled like a serpent around the whole world. And by the banks of that river, there he found the three Terrible Women all asleep beneath a poplar tree, with the dead poplar leaves lying all about them. Their golden wings were folded and their brass claws were crossed, and two of them slept with their hideous heads beneath their wings like birds, and the serpents in their hair writhed out from under the feathers of gold. But the youngest slept between her two sisters, and she lay on her back, with her beautiful sad face turned to the sky; and though she slept her eyes were wide open. If the boy had seen her, he would have been changed into stone by the terror and the pity of it, she was so awful; but he had thought of a plan for killing her without looking at her face.

As soon as he caught sight of the three from far off, he took his shining shield from his shoulders, and held it up like a mirror, so that he saw the Dreadful Women reflected in it, and did not see the Terrible Head itself. Then he came nearer and nearer, till he reckoned that he was within a sword's stroke of the youngest, and he guessed where he should strike a back blow behind him. Then he drew the Sword of Sharpness and struck once, and the Terrible Head was cut from the shoulders of the creature, and the blood leaped out and struck him like a blow. But he thrust the Terrible Head into his wallet, and flew away without looking behind.

The two Dreadful Sisters who were left wakened, and rose in the air like great birds; and though they could not see him because of his Cap of Darkness, they flew after him up the wind, following by the scent through the clouds, like hounds hunting in a wood. They came so close that he could hear the clattering of their golden wings, and their shrieks to each other: 'Here, here.' 'No, there; this way he went,' as they chased him. But the Shoes of Swiftness flew too fast for them, and at last their cries and the rattle of their wings died away as he crossed the great river that runs around the world.

When the horrible creatures were far in the distance, and the boy found himself on the right side of the river, he flew straight eastward, seeking his own country. But, as he looked down from the air, he saw a very strange sight – a beautiful girl chained to a stake at the high-water mark of the sea. The girl was so frightened or so tired that she was only prevented from falling by the iron chain around her waist, and there she hung, as if she were dead. The boy was very sorry for her, and flew down and stood beside her. When he spoke she raised her head but his voice only seemed to frighten her. Then he remembered that he was wearing the Cap of Darkness, and that she could only hear him, not see him. So he took it off, and there he stood before her, the handsomest young man she had ever seen in all her life, with short curly yellow hair, and blue eyes, and a laughing face. And he thought her the most beautiful girl in the world. With one blow of the Sword of Sharpness he cut the iron chain that bound her, and then he asked her why she was here, and why men treated her so cruelly.

She told him that she was the daughter of the King of that country, and that she was tied there to be eaten by a monstrous beast out of the sea; for the beast came and devoured a girl every day. Now the lot had fallen on her; and, as she was just saying this, a long fierce head of a cruel sea-creature rose out of the waves and snapped at her. But the beast had been too greedy and too hurried, so he missed his aim the first time. Before he could rise and bite again, the boy had whipped the Terrible Head out of his wallet and held it up. And when the sea beast leaped out once more its eyes fell on the head, and instantly it was turned into a stone. And the stone beast is there on the sea-coast to this day.

Then the boy and the girl went to the palace of

the King, her father, where everyone was weeping for her death, and they could hardly believe their eyes when they saw her come back well. And the King and Queen made much of the boy, and could not contain themselves for delight when they found he wanted to marry their daughter. So the two were married with the most splendid rejoicings, and when they had passed some time at court they went home in a ship to the boy's own country. He could not carry his bride through the air, so he took the Shoes of Swiftness and the Cap of Darkness and the Sword of Sharpness up to a lonely place in the hills. There he left them, and there they were found by the man and woman who had met him at home beside the sea, and had helped him to start on his journey.

When this had been done, the boy and his bride set forth for home, and landed at the harbour of his native land. But whom should he meet in the very street of the town but his own mother, flying for her life from the wicked King, who now wished to kill her because he found that she would never marry him! For if she had liked the King little before, she liked him far worse now that he had caused her son to disappear so suddenly. She did not know, of course, where the boy had gone, but thought the King had slain him secretly. So now she was running for her very life, and the wicked King was following her with a sword in his hand. Then, behold! She ran into her son's very arms, but he only had time to kiss her and step in front of her, when the King struck at him with his sword. The boy caught the blow on his shield, and cried to the King:

'I swore to bring you the Terrible Head, and see how I keep my oath!'

Then he drew forth the head from his wallet, and when the King's eyes fell on it, instantly he was turned to stone, just as he stood there with his sword lifted!

Now all the people rejoiced, because the wicked King should rule them no longer. And they asked the boy to be their king, but he said no, he must take his mother home to her father's house. So the people chose for King the man who had been kind to the boy's mother when first she was cast on the island in the great chest.

Presently the boy and his mother and his wife set sail for his mother's own country, from which she had been driven so unkindly. But on the way they stayed at the court of a King, and it happened that he was holding games, and giving prizes to the best runners, boxers and quoit-throwers. Then the boy would try his strength with the rest, but he threw the quoit so far that it went beyond what had ever been thrown before, and fell in the crowd, striking a man so that he died. Now this man was no other than the father of the boy's mother, who had fled away from his own kingdom for fear his grandson should find him and kill him after all. Thus he was destroyed by his own cowardice and by chance, and thus the prophecy was fulfilled. But the boy and his wife and his mother went back to the kingdom that was theirs, and lived long and happily after all their troubles.

FINIS